The Suited Hippy and the Stress Junkie

About the Authors

Our greatest fears can bring our greatest gifts.

It's difficult facing our fears and there are many ways we try to escape them. That could be with alcohol, avoidance tactics or over-work. However, if we are not careful, our fears can control us and rob us of our freedom and joy. If we are open to looking inside and facing them, then we gain insights into who we really are and we can shine the light for others.

SEBASTIAN ADAMS

Sebastian is a CTI-trained coach, artist and author. His coaching approach is holistic and he draws on different mind and energy tools, including somatics, EFT and hypnotherapy.

Sebastian's art is based on embodying an intention into an abstract oil painting. His work can be found at

www.emotionscapes.com

The common theme of all of his creative output is to help transform people's lives.

JOANNA KANE

Joanna is a personal and leadership development coach (CTI trained), speaker and author. She has worked with individuals and teams for many years helping them 'shine their light' and release their potential.

Joanna is particularly passionate about women's leadership and helping women find balance and fulfilment in their lives.

Joanna and Sebastian are the co-founders of Trailblazers, an organisation that provides personal, team and leadership development.

www.thetrailblazers.co.uk

SEBASTIAN ADAMS &

JOANNA KANE

First published in 2014 by Reed McKenna Publishing Ltd

Ordering Information:
Special discounts are available on quantity purchases by corporations, associations, educators, and others. For details, contact the publisher at corpsales@ reedmckenna.com.

US & UK trade bookstores and wholesalers:
Contact stores@reedmckenna.com

To all those who have supported us and encouraged us along the way.

Prologue

Her eyes barely open, the bright lights blurring past, Germaine stifled a yawn that became a sob. 'I'm so tired,' she thought. At that moment her supposedly liberating Mercedes sports car felt more like a prison, a symbol of her self-imposed incarceration.

'It's not worth it!' she screamed at the unhearing drivers around her. 'I can't take it any more!'

As she entered the elevated section of the Hammersmith flyover, a voice in her head taunted her, 'What if you were just to jerk the steering wheel so the car hits the central reservation?'

Germaine became acutely aware of her hands on the grey leather; it was as if the wheel was pressing against her flesh. The tension in her shoulders was building, stressing her awareness that a small movement, voluntary or not, could offer her a way out.

An urgent beep from her mobile on the passenger seat brought her back to conscious awareness. A glance at the neon blue of the dashboard clock told her she was late, again. The moment had passed, leaving a gap somewhere inside of her.

~ 1 ~

The insistent triple beep of the alarm roused Germaine from her hard-fought-for sleep. She'd only managed to fall asleep about an hour and a half ago, but it felt like ten minutes. She wanted to turn the world off, just for a while.

Then she remembered all the things she needed to do and all the things she hadn't done. The panic swamped her; there was no refuge. Zombie-like, she hauled her legs from under the duvet and placed her feet tentatively on the carpet, as if testing whether it would support her. There was no sign her boyfriend Ben had even registered the alarm as he hadn't moved, which made her even more discontented.

She dragged herself wearily to the bathroom and started her auto-pilot preparations for the day.

Ten minutes in a scalding shower.

Ten minutes scrabbling in her closet for something half respectable to wear to the office. She realised with a groan that it needed to be extra formal as a banking client services director was coming in for a pre-pitch meeting. And her shoes didn't match...

Five minutes drying her hair – make that ten minutes this morning, noticing how baggy her eyes were, necessitating an emergency application of eye cream.

A quick glance at her watch showed she was late... again. She hurtled for the door, skipping breakfast... again. It was going to be far easier to grab a coffee and something from the fridge at work.

Germaine was not generally an unhappy person. She had what she considered a good life: great friends, a supportive boyfriend, a well-paid job doing something she enjoyed, a two-bedroom flat overlooking Chiswick Green and a Mercedes SLK sports car. But something just wasn't right. She wasn't sleeping, and she was starting to resent the people at work, her boyfriend and even the success she had worked so hard for.

'What's wrong with me? Why aren't I happy with what I've got?' she thought as she hurtled into work, applying patches of eye liner and lipstick at tactical traffic stops, bringing the occasional toot of annoyance or amusement from other drivers.

Luckily this morning no one had blocked her access to that most prized of all London perks: a parking spot at work. That meant she didn't have the hassle of getting security to call the unsuspecting offender to move... again.

Smiling a greeting to the new receptionist, Angela or whatever her name was, Germaine landed at her desk and ducked behind her computer screen. Outlook glared in bold that she had 112 new messages. She'd left her iPhone on charge at the office so she hadn't been checking emails the evening before, and this was the price she paid. She scanned the contents of her inbox, ignoring those that were personal or informational, looking for messages from the MD, her clients, the other board members and her team, in that order.

Copia was a new, dynamic advertising agency that was starting to punch well above its weight. Its funky open-plan offices were great for creating the feeling of a non-hierarchical and collaborative workplace, but there were disadvantages. Where people were positioned had a dramatic impact on their effectiveness. Poor Ellie, wedged in between the toilets and the photocopier, was a case in point. She was a trainee account handler, fresh from college, and she didn't look happy.

With a quick glance at the Digital Design of the Year award perched on her partition, Germaine began a quick reply to Rich Evans, head of advertising at Gintech, a potentially lucrative global campaign. Rich's email was direct, but Germaine sensed a slight flirtation in its tone, although nothing she could pinpoint definitively. While he was attractive and had a certain charm, she didn't have the energy to entertain such thoughts, except on the rare nights when she got blasted with Samantha Leeson, her best friend from college.

In the past five years Germaine had risen through the ranks to become director of client services. She was on the board, reporting directly to the MD and owner, Jeremy Horn. The company had since gone from strength to strength, acquiring a number of prestigious clients and winning sought-after awards, although that provided her with surprisingly little satisfaction. Instead, her success only gave her a sense of carrying a greater and greater burden.

Owen Wilcox smiled at her and made the universal hand gesture for coffee. She nodded and rose to accompany him to the kitchen. Five years her junior, he was a senior account director with a great track record and an easy manner that endeared him to practically everyone. He always looked bright-eyed and full of self-confidence. Germaine was his direct boss, but he made her feel a bit disconcerted.

'Sleep better last night?' he asked, looking concerned.

'I'm fine, but coffee's a great idea. How are things with Lee Edwards?' Germaine steered the conversation onto a business path where she felt more stable.

'I haven't spoken to Mike this morning, but I left him a message last night. Are you worried about something?'

'No, nothing specific. I just know it's coming up to budget approval for those guys and we don't want to take our eye off the ball. I know Mike is saying all the right things and they've been happy with what we've done for them up to now, but I'm less sure of Lee and I suspect he has more influence than you think.'

'Perhaps you're right.' Owen looked away briefly and made a move towards the coffee machine. 'Your regular?' He selected a decaf capsule for himself and a double espresso for Germaine.

Germaine noticed he looked a little disengaged.

'OK, I guess you're right. I need to take a chill pill!' She noticed that her neck was stiff and tried to release her shoulders.

Owen nodded and said, 'I'll make a courtesy call to Lee this afternoon. He's in their board meeting this morning.'

Her heart jumped. 'Shit, the board meeting... sorry, Owen, need to go.' She grabbed the coffee and scuttled back to her desk to pick up her phone and papers before rushing to the boardroom.

~ 2 ~

Mike Lessing, the financial director, was focused on the large whiteboard at the end of the room. In his early fifties, he was of average height and going grey. Many hours of sitting behind a desk had softened his frame, although not his will or his mind. Germaine never felt entirely at ease around him, as if he might find fault with her at any moment.

Following his gaze she saw that Jeremy was holding court in front of an organisation diagram featuring the name of Livko, one of her major accounts, in big red letters. She quickly scanned the picture for its meaning. Beside 'marketing director' was written 'Dom'. Dominic Fox was Copia's creative and planning director, whose reputation for strategic and creative flair was only bested by his opinion of himself. Liam, the account manager, had his name written in green with a question mark just below and to the right of the brand manager for the client.

'Ah, you're nearly on time. Glad you could make it,' quipped Jeremy to Germaine and Tom Hennessy, the marketing director, who went to sit down next to him.

'So what's on the agenda?' Tom began chirpily.

Jeremy ignored the question and asked, 'Where's Dom?'

'He's probably double booked,' said Mike.

Germaine saw Jeremy frown and wondered whether that was about Dominic or Mike.

'Well, he'll just have to remain in the dark,' said Jeremy, pointedly looking around the table. 'First there's the matter of the strategic offsite. I think it would be good to split it into two parts. The morning for us – perhaps at Soho

House? – then the afternoon with some of our key managers to get clear on the priorities for the following year. Your thoughts?'

'I'm worried about asking only a few of the managers to the meeting. You know some of them can get a bit sensitive if they feel they're being excluded,' Tom offered.

'Nonsense, that's what leadership is about. You make clear decisions that people can follow. If you start to mollycoddle employees you end up not being able to make any decisions. You're good at pacifying, find some way of spinning it so that they see sense,' was Jeremy's reply.

Mike leaned forward with his eyes down. 'Taking everyone offsite in the current climate just isn't practical, they'll understand,' he said.

Jeremy looked over to Germaine and she realised her attention had wandered. She wanted to say that she didn't care, but she couldn't. 'We could all go for a beer afterwards so they get to know what's going on, and it's informal,' she said spontaneously, then shrank inwardly. Why did she say that? Another drinking session was the last thing she needed.

'Great idea, that ticks the boxes,' said Jeremy. 'We could go to the Lamb and Calf, is that cheap enough for you, Mike? Now, talking of drinks, I've been doing some thinking about Livko.'

'Here we go,' thought Germaine, tensing at the mention of her client.

'We need to up our game,' he went on. 'I've heard Hawes and Smith have been sniffing around the account, which as you know is potentially our biggest. I'm not sure we're entrenched enough. They liked our ideas on the vodka pitch, but I don't get the feeling they're entirely confident in us.'

Germaine felt as if her stomach had dropped six inches and the colour drained from her face.

At that moment the door swung open and in burst Dominic. Looking around with a smile on his face, his eyes momentarily lingered on the whiteboard and he aimed a conspiratorial wink at Germaine. 'I see you're talking about Livko. Guess who I was out with last night?'

Germaine leaned forward, noticing that Tom and Jeremy did likewise. Dominic chuckled wryly while shaking his head, a characteristic gesture that let his audience know an amusing story was forthcoming.

'I was supposed to be meeting Ben – you know, Ben Tyler from LND,' began Dom, 'but unfortunately he had to cry off, something about getting grief for not remembering his girlfriend's birthday. So there I was, enjoying a quiet jar in Tyros, when there was a tap on my shoulder and blow me down if it wasn't Simon Levvy, the brand manager from Livko.' The others laughed at his fake East End accent.

'He'd had a couple of sherbets by the look of him, so I asked him to pull up a pew and we got to talking and drinking,' Dom continued. 'He's quite an entertaining guy when you get to know him. I found out loads of stuff about his family, he's very well connected, and apparently Livko have introduced a fast-track talent development programme. They've brought in a guy called Theo Britten, aka The Suited Hippy. I'm not sure what he does, but Si has been selected for the programme and is pretty pumped about working with him. Apparently there's a rumour that Livko are looking to acquire the Dark Horse vodka brand and Si is being positioned as marketing manager for the combined portfolio.'

'This is what Liam should be doing, finding out stuff like this, but he's not up to it,' Jeremy butted in angrily.

Tom looked across at Germaine, who had the sinking feeling she was in the hot seat again. She had only just promoted Liam to senior account manager, based on the fact that he was reliable, consistent and had a track record of delivering results, but she knew Jeremy thought he was too inexperienced.

'He's a good worker,' Germaine said defensively. The implied criticism of her management had put her on the spot and her mind had gone blank. 'We just need to give him time...'

'We need someone with charisma and drive handling that account, especially with its growing importance.' Jeremy cut her off. 'As you've got a personal relationship there, Dom, I want you to keep your hand in. Which senior account manager would do a good job?'

'I'm not sure Liam would take too kindly to being swapped out,' Tom injected in a measured tone.

'I'm not talking about swapping him out, maybe putting someone else in with him. We could position it within the context of the impending acquisitions,' suggested Jeremy.

Germaine started to feel her hackles rise. Bloody alpha males, they still felt they had to decide things for her. 'Now hold on a minute, I don't want to make any snap changes,' she interjected. 'I will get more involved in the account and make sure Liam doesn't drop any balls.'

'It'll be on your head,' said Jeremy, looking disappointed.

There was an uncomfortable silence for a second or two, then he changed the subject to one of his pet hates, employees using the internet for personal use. With a collective groan, the board began a debate over the ins and outs of blocking, filtering, eavesdropping on the various social networking sites and so on.

It was twenty-five minutes later before Mike was finally able to chime in with, 'I've got to head out in five minutes for a meeting with our accounting firm. Do we have a clear set of actions this time?'

'Weren't you taking notes?' asked Jeremy sarcastically. 'I thought that would be right up your street.'

'I have taken notes, actually, and if you want I'll distribute them by email,' Mike told him.

'Works for me.' Jeremy nodded, stood up, picked up his laptop and phone and left the room.

Tom, Germaine and Dominic remained seated for a second, not quite sure what had just happened.

~ 3 ~

'I wish Jeremy wouldn't put you on the spot like that,' said Tom as they left the boardroom.

'I need some air, fancy a quick coffee?' replied Germaine.

On the way they stopped at Chloe's desk. With her long chestnut hair, sultry eyes and model's pout, Jeremy's PA wouldn't have looked out of place as the face of a cosmetics company, although she was anything but a trophy. She was good at her job and wouldn't let anyone forget it.

'Can you check Jeremy's diary next week, Thursday or Friday, for a meeting with me, James and that potential PR chap... what's his name? Jeremy will know who I mean,' said Germaine.

'Thursday 3–4 pm any good? Or Friday any time between 10 am and 2:30.' Chloe smiled. 'Mark Anderson is the PR guy I think you mean.'

'That's him, thank you, Chloe.' Germaine checked her iPhone to see which slot she had available and saw a text from her friend Sam. She ignored it and selected a time. 'Friday 2 pm?'

'It's in his diary.'

'Great.' Germaine went to leave, then on a whim turned back and asked, 'What's he doing after 2:30, by the way?'

'Not sure, it's just been marked as in a meeting.' Chloe's expression made it clear no further information was going to be forthcoming.

'Dixies?' Tom and Germaine both said spontaneously as they walked away.

Germaine visited the café so often she was considered almost family – which of course meant that Stefano, the owner, thought she needed fattening up. That gave her the tricky job of maintaining both a slim figure and a cake habit. The staff at Dixies somehow believed her to be uniquely qualified as tester of new concoctions and, if she happened to be in the café towards the end of the day, a cake disposal unit.

'So, Tom, tell me what happened in that meeting,' she began when they'd sat down.

'I think there was a bit of manoeuvring, but I'm not sure for what or why. Mike's always got a secret agenda, although you'll never get it out of him. He's too smart for his own good sometimes.'

'He and Jeremy are either as thick as thieves or at each other's throats. Jeremy keeps changing his mind and doesn't tell me what's going on.'

'Don't worry, it's not just you,' said Tom ruefully.

Germaine laughed. 'How's the move?'

'We're in now, thank God. Can't wait to get everything out of boxes, though. The worst bit was the mortgage. Our lenders pulled out at the last moment and in the end we settled for a five-year fixed rate. The interest was quite a bit higher, but at least we know where we stand for a while. How about you, has Ben moved in yet?'

'Yep, he finally sold his Camden flat. He's committed now,' said Germaine, making a face.

'Hey, it's what you wanted and he's a great guy,' said Tom, smiling. 'And he couldn't have a better girl. You're brilliant... but I do worry about you sometimes.'

'No need, I can look after myself.'

Tom leaned back in his chair, looking affronted.

'Don't take things so personally,' said Germaine, trying to appease him. 'I guess we both need to be a bit more vocal at board meetings.'

Tom looked a little perplexed, but he didn't comment.

~ 4 ~

Germaine had organised her weekly team meeting on the same day as the board meeting so she could relay any missives from the gods on high. Once everyone had sat down and the customary chatter had died down, she began.

'OK, let's keep this as brief as possible, I know we've all got a lot of stuff to do. First, on a positive note, as part of our company planning day we're arranging an evening drinks do. They're talking The Lamb and Calf, but I think suggestions for an alternative venue and ways of making the event fun might be welcome. Any ideas?'

'Let's have it somewhere cool for a change,' said Katherine, who had a devilish streak despite her almost gamine appearance. 'What about one of the bars in Hoxton? I know it's a bit of a cab ride away, but it would make a change from the usual.'

Owen laughed. 'I like your thinking. I can picture Mike now, ordering a round of Red Stripes, chuffed at how little the damage is while his credit card's being cloned.'

A debate began about how edgy Hoxton actually was, but Germaine brought them back on topic. 'We don't have to sort it right now, so think about it. Now, I wouldn't mind a quick catch-up on accounts.'

She worked round the table, asking each individual account manager what was happening and probing for details on their clients. When it came to Liam, she could feel her attitude changing. Instead of continuing the review format, she jumped straight in.

'Livko has become a bit of a hot topic, Liam. Dominic had a chance meeting with Simon Levvy and there's some potential movement in the account. Had you heard?'

Liam looked worried and visibly shrank. 'Er, to be honest, no.'

'I guess it's not public knowledge. When's the last time you spoke to Simon?'

'A couple of days ago, we chatted about the artwork for the Easter campaign. He said he was happy with the design, just asked for a couple of tweaks, and wanted to know if I was available next week to show it to their strategy director. Why, what's happening?'

'A potential merger and a bit of competition, as far as I can tell. I think you and I need to sit down with Dominic to discuss it further.'

'If you like I could do a bit of digging, if it would be of any help,' Owen offered.

'Depends on how you ask. If it's sensitive I wouldn't want us causing Simon any trouble. Liam, do you think he would be open to talking to you about it?'

Liam looked unsure, so to defuse the tension Germaine moved on. 'Let's talk about it later. Who's up for a quick drink after work? We still haven't celebrated Katherine's birthday from last week, or the success of the Lions campaign.'

There was a unanimous show of hands, with a few 'I can only do a couple' remarks.

Later that afternoon, Tom strolled up to Germaine's desk looking rather pleased with himself. 'I've been doing a bit of research on that Theo Britten,' he told her.

'Who?' Germaine asked distractedly as another text beeped on her phone.

'You know, the chap Dominic mentioned in the board meeting.'

'The guy who's helping out at Livko? What does he do again?'

'Apparently he's a coach.'

'Like a personal trainer?'

'Yep, except it's more to do with the mind as far as I can tell. It looks like he's worked with some pretty interesting people.'

Germaine read the text, which was from Sam again: 'Don't ignore me!!' Scrolling back, she saw that the previous message was: 'Still fancy the flix on Fri?'

'Excuse me a sec, Tom, I just need to send a couple of texts.'

Sam was undeniably Germaine's best friend. They'd pretty much hit it off from day one at college. Sam, a couple of years older, had tucked Germaine firmly under her wing and guided her safely through freshers' week and the first year. A feisty Scot with an eye for a deal and a taste for Chablis, Sam had turned her back on creative life after college and gone over to the dark side – sales, and even worse, financial sales, much to the dismay of many of her peers. It had the handy side effect that, as an outsider who knew the advertising game but wasn't involved, she could give Germaine the benefit of her opinion, although her objectivity tended to get sidelined depending on the volume of alcohol consumed and whether arrogant men were involved.

'Checking with Ben,' Germaine deftly thumbed to Sam, then immediately conjured up another text to Ben: 'Hi hon, do we have plans on Fri?'

'Anyway, back to Theo Britten,' said Tom when she'd finished. 'I've sent you a couple of links, which make quite interesting reading.'

'OK, will do. Thanks,' said Germaine. She watched Tom as he left and saw him stop to have a quick word with Ellie, the new graduate.

Germaine glanced at the office clock and then her phone.

'You busy?' asked Jeremy, catching her by surprise. He beckoned her over.

'Sure, what's up?' said Germaine, aware that several people had glanced up.

'I want to run something by you. Let's go to the board-room,' said Jeremy, who was also aware they were being watched. 'I've been doing a bit of digging,' he added, talking as they walked.

'Digging? For what, bodies?' Germaine quipped and immediately wished she hadn't.

As they entered the boardroom, Jeremy continued, 'In a manner of speaking. I was doing a bit of market research and looking at reviewing our search consultancy, when up popped that guy Theo Britten. You know, the one Dominic mentioned. One thing led to another and I had a chat with Nigel about him.'

Theo Britten again. Why was he suddenly on everyone's radar?

'Nigel, our search guy?' she asked. 'What's he got to do with Theo?'

'I think I'm going to hire Theo Britten to do some coaching,' Jeremy went on.

'You're getting coached?' Germaine asked, incredulous.

'Maybe, but I'm looking to offer it to all our directors and senior managers. I want someone to give it a go first... and I thought of you.'

Germaine's stomach squirmed. 'Why did you think of me? What would it be for?'

'Well, to be honest you seem a bit stressed sometimes and you know I'm not good at that type of thing.'

'You mean you can't stand the thought of me bursting into tears on you,' said Germaine, trying to keep her cool.

'Something like that.' Jeremy laughed. 'Look, I'd just like you to check it out and see if it's something you would like – no commitment. You only have to have a chat with the guy.'

'No harm in that. When are you thinking?'

'Well, I got Chloe to check your diaries and you're both free tomorrow at 10. I've asked her to drop you an invite with his details. Is that OK?'

'What if I'd said no?' Germaine asked.

'Why would you?' he shrugged.

~ 5 ~

A few manic hours on the phone and several meetings later, Germaine took a deep breath and looked up at the clock, the conversation with Jeremy continuing to buzz in her head. It was approaching 6:30 and everyone around her was still busy.

'Jeez, I need a drink,' she announced. 'Let's get out of here before Mike assumes we're staying for the night and locks us in. I'll stump up for the first three bottles of Veuve, but beyond that you're on your own.'

Katherine made a show of pressing a key on her keyboard as if to say SEND and got up with a sigh. 'I'll be right with you, my work is done!'

Owen was having a chat with a couple of junior creatives, but he signalled he'd be with them in five minutes. Liam looked unsure.

'Beer o'clock?' asked Dominic as he walked past her desk.

'Certainly is, but you can have the beer – we'll be drinking champagne!'

Dominic took her arm in his and escorted her towards the exit, closely followed by her team.

A couple of hours and a few glasses of bubbly later, Germaine exited from Turnham Green tube, having left her car at work. She was knackered but buoyed up by the alcohol. Dominic and Owen had been entertaining her, but towards the end she had started to tune out and decided to call it a day and leave the kids to play.

Walking along the terrace, she became aware of someone standing in a shady doorway. She shivered and picked up her step, pulling her handbag and coat closer.

There were a few people up ahead and as she turned to see across the road, she caught a glimpse of the figure from the doorway crossing the street and looking back at her, his face obscured by his hoodie. His hands deep in the pocket of his baggy jeans, he stopped on the opposite pavement and stood facing her.

Germaine's heart was beating hard. What was he doing?

There was a bar behind him. The door opened to let someone out and she could hear the music.

She walked even more quickly, but the man was matching her pace on the other side of the road. Remembering there was a pub at the end of the street, Germaine started to jog. Then, sensing a presence behind her, she began to run.

A young girl came out of the pub ahead; a few seconds later an older man followed. They were both surprised to see Germaine running towards them. She stopped, her heart thumping, and turned, raising her arm in a half-hearted gesture of defence. She expected to see her pursuer frozen in the act of chasing her, but he wasn't there.

'You OK?' asked the older man, looking at her closely. 'You need some help?'

'There was a guy... there was a guy following me, chasing me,' she said, barely able to speak.

'Shall we call the police? Did he hurt you?'

'No, no, I'm fine. Nothing happened.'

'Where do you live?' the girl asked.

'It's OK, I'm nearly home,' said Germaine, sobered up by the episode.

Reflecting on it later with Ben, she wondered if she hadn't been a little paranoid. Had the man really been chasing her? She couldn't be sure.

~ 6 ~

The following day, Germaine dashed out of the office on her way to meet Theo Britten at Dixies. She was ten minutes late – not a good start.

She spotted a man watching her from a table in the corner of the café. He had cropped blond hair and was wearing an open-necked lilac shirt. When he stood and moved around the table towards Germaine, she could see he was also wearing smart grey jeans and black shoes.

'You must be Germaine,' he said, enfolding her hand in a warm, firm handshake. She was held by his cool blue eyes, which dominated his Nordic features.

'And I assume you're Theo?' she said, composing herself.

'Take a pew,' he answered, pointing at a comfortable armchair. As they sat she noticed a picture on the wall of a Japanese garden in pastel greens. Funny, she'd been at that table so many times but never really clocked that.

Theo pointed to a half-finished breakfast smoothie on the table and asked what she would like.

'They'll bring me my coffee – as you might guess I'm a regular here,' she said, smiling. 'Sorry I'm late, I had difficulty getting out of the office.'

'Not a problem. I was enjoying checking out your habitat.'

The barista brought over Germaine's latte. 'Here you go. No muffins this morning?'

'Not this morning, thanks,' she mumbled.

'So how much has Jeremy told you about what I do and why he got in contact?' asked Theo, taking a slow sip of his drink.

'Not much, really. I heard you assist people with their management skills and help teams improve their performance.'

'So he didn't tell you very much. That must have left you a bit curious and a bit cautious too.'

'You could say that, yes. I must admit I was slightly concerned that this might be seen as a negative thing. I'm delivering results and so are my team, so why me?'

'It's interesting that you think coaching is for people who are not delivering. Coaching can be useful in that area, but most of the coaches I know work with those who would actually be classified as high potentials. Coaching can assist them with meeting some key challenges head on, helping them close the gap between where they are now and where they would like to be. It also helps them understand more about themselves and how they work with others. This is pretty crucial stuff for those who are in leadership roles or aspiring leaders.'

Germaine felt more at ease. She liked the relaxed way he explained things.

'Would it be useful for you to find out a bit more about how I work? Or we can start with me understanding a little more about you and what's going on in your world,' Theo continued.

She didn't feel quite ready to open up to a stranger, so she asked him to carry on.

'OK, fundamentally I help people understand themselves, what makes them tick, what their vision is, what they're here for... that type of thing.'

'That sounds a bit lofty.' Germaine laughed somewhat nervously.

'I like to think of it as an inside-out process, where we work on your interior landscape first, because that's where

I believe the real change happens. That way you start getting more of the results you want in the real world. You're far more in charge of creating your reality than you realise – we all are.'

Germaine shifted uncomfortably. The thought of digging around in her 'interior landscape' didn't exactly fill her with joy. She could feel a tightening around her jawline and she knew she was frowning.

'The process usually takes around six months,' Theo added. 'I only work with people who are ready to go on this journey. You have to choose it, as it requires you to be open and prepared to challenge the way you think and behave.'

'What do you mean?' asked Germaine.

'Most of us operate on autopilot. We do things because that's what we've always done and that's what got us to where we are. But where we are is not where we were and what worked in the past might not work now. This is one of the key challenges leaders and managers face, especially when moving between roles and companies. There's so much "doing" that there's precious little time left for just "being".'

It hit Germaine that her whole life felt like she was on autopilot, but at the same time she was getting a bit frustrated about all the tasks she had waiting for her in the office.

'At the moment I'm struggling to keep on top of everything with the day job, let alone to think about adding to my list of things to do,' she said.

'How do you know when you're stressed?' Theo asked her.

'I feel panicky, short-fused and erratic, and ultimately I shut down.'

He nodded, reached for a pen and started to draw a picture on his pad. It was a stick bridge with a couple of cars on it.

'Excuse the quality of the drawing. If you look at stress from an engineering perspective, say with this bridge, with a light load of cars the bridge is quite happy.' He began to scribble again. 'If you take the bridge to the maximum loading it's designed for, what do you think will happen?'

'It will fall down?'

Theo smiled. 'Only if the designer was bad at his job. No, it's designed for that maximum load, so you shouldn't see anything.' He added another box to the bridge drawing. 'But add just a little more than it's built for and what do you think happens then?'

'It starts to strain, I guess.'

'Exactly. It will begin to creak and cracks will appear. What do you think will happen if that continues?'

'Then it will fall down.'

'And what can you do to stop that?'

'Take off some of the traffic.'

'What else?'

'Strengthen the bridge.'

'That's one way of putting it.'

'So what you're saying is I need to get stronger or reduce my workload?' asked Germaine.

'Another way of saying strengthen the bridge is to say add more support for the bridge.' With a few strokes, Theo thickened the pillars under the bridge in his drawing. 'The concept of stress on our bodies is the same, except the creaks and cracks show up as feelings and behaviours. They are the signs that tell us we're overloaded. If it's a small amount for a short duration, it's probably not going to worry us. However, if it's either a great deal more than we can handle or it's over a sustained period, the signs will be more severe and eventually the situation will lead to a breakdown of some sort.'

'Why are you telling me this?' asked Germaine, feeling defensive.

'The coaching process can help on both fronts, by providing you with support in getting you where you want to go and by helping you find ways to lighten your load. Does that make sense to you?'

'Yes, I think so, but I'm not sure how it might work.'

'Well, I'll explain the process a bit,' said Theo. 'For me to take you on as a client I need two things: I need you to be as honest as possible with me and with yourself, and I need you to do your best to honour the commitments you make in the sessions.'

'And what do you do?' asked Germaine.

'What I offer in return is to help you clarify and move towards your goals or vision, and to support you on the way to realising them. I will be 100% on your side, always. I'm here to hold up a mirror to challenge your thinking and your actions. We waste so much energy on thoughts and actions that do not support us and what we want to achieve. By getting clear on what we want and choosing what we do and how we do it, we become much more efficient and effective. Changing the way we think and behave is not always simple, and having someone to champion us through the process can help to lighten the load. Does that make things clearer?'

Germaine nodded.

'As far as the nuts and bolts of the process go,' he went on, 'typically we would have seven coaching sessions, two in the first month then one a month. Before that I would suggest some 360-degree feedback.'

'I've heard of that. What exactly is involved?' asked Germaine.

'I would canvass your peers, Jeremy and some of your team to get feedback on your strengths, areas for development and your overall impact. Most of us are so busy getting on with the job that we don't take the time to ask for feedback to help us improve, or give it to other people. You, Jeremy and I would then have a three-way meeting to get clear on the objectives of the coaching, followed by another three-way meeting at the end to gauge its success and whether any further action is required. How does that sound?'

Germaine realised she'd been staring at his neck, in particular at his small, fishhook-like pendant. Slightly startled, she piped up, 'I guess that all sounds fine, but I'm not sure what we'd talk about.'

Theo angled his head slightly. 'I'm curious, what do you love about what you do?'

Germaine took a moment to think. 'I love the diversity, all the great people I work with, the characters in the business. I know it sounds clichéd, but we really do work hard and play hard... and the money's good,' she admitted reluctantly.

Leaning forward slightly, Theo asked, 'I hear a lot about working hard and playing hard in business at the moment. What does that look like?'

'Well, I do a fair amount of client entertainment at bars and restaurants. We also burn the midnight oil quite a bit, especially at pitch time. It's expected and it's part of the job.'

Germaine noticed Theo raising an eyebrow briefly when she continued, 'Actually it seems to be more difficult for me to do these days. Maybe it's something to do with hitting thirty, but I definitely notice I need longer to recover now.'

'If you do decide you want to work with me and are prepared to invest your time in this process, I'm wondering, what might success look like for you now? What do you really want now?' Theo probed.

Germaine was a bit thrown by the sudden turn of the questioning. 'I haven't really thought about that.' She sat back in her chair, tugging at her earring. 'I've been so busy I feel like a hamster on a wheel, never knowing how to get off.'

She put her hands in her lap and looked into his eyes. 'I guess success might be having a supportive boss who trusts me, a team that's performing well and me sleeping better.'

With the words came a welling of emotion, which she struggled desperately to keep down. It felt like the pressure building in her stomach and chest was clamping her throat in a vice-like grip.

Theo looked at her with compassion for a few moments, then breathed deeply and rolled back his shoulders. Watching him seemed to break the grip on her throat, and Germaine too breathed deeply, a tickling sensation rising from her neck up through the right side of her head.

'If you did have a supportive boss and a team that was performing well, what would you be feeling? What would be different for you?' he continued.

'I guess I wouldn't feel so fuzzy, on shaky ground and not in control.' She could hardly believe she was saying that – was it how she really felt? Strangely the room felt a little more spacious and she was aware she'd taken another deep breath.

'Good, we can have fun with that,' said Theo. 'Anyway, I would love to work with you. You are in the perfect place. The next step is for you to choose whether you would like to experience a coaching programme.'

'I think it could be good for me, but I need a bit of time to think about it,' said Germaine, although she knew her mind was already made up. Something about Theo's non-judgemental demeanour made her feel relaxed and at ease. It had been a surprising meeting.

'Have a chat with Jeremy and if you decide to go ahead, we can get the initial three-way meeting underway in the next week or so. It's been a pleasure chatting with you,' said Theo. They said their goodbyes and he strolled out of the café.

Germaine sat and thought for a while. She felt different, and that in itself was curious.

'Another latte?' asked the barista, breaking her reverie.

'Umm, actually no, not at the moment, thanks. I'd better be getting back,' she said as she got up, picking up her phone and bag. Theo had left his card. Picking it up, she could see that on the back was a picture of a butterfly bathed in sunlight, and a quote: 'What the caterpillar calls the end, the rest of the world calls a butterfly. Lao Tzu'.

Germaine pocketed the card and walked slowly back to the office.

~ 7 ~

After taking a sleeping pill in a desperate attempt to get a decent night's sleep, the following morning Germaine had been dreaming she was caught with her knickers down when the toilet door on a commuter train opened, leaving her exposed to a group of laughing businessmen. The alarm was the panic button she'd pressed in an attempt to close the door.

Heart pounding and head thumping, she didn't see the funny side. Five hours of sleep had been the best of the week, but after dragging herself out of bed and looking in the bathroom mirror, her spirits sank.

'Jeez, look at my eyes,' she thought. 'Those bloody lines. That's not me. I'm only 32, not 42!'

She fought back the tears, which would just make the situation worse.

She heard Ben getting out of bed and coming to the bathroom. 'Can I come in? I need a wee,' he said in a sleepy voice.

Germaine quickly splashed cold water on her face and ducked into the shower. For some reason that she didn't understand, she didn't want Ben to see her this way.

As he proceeded to relieve himself, Ben glanced at Germaine in the shower. 'I think I might join you,' he said, obviously feeling perky.

'You can have it now, I've got to get ready,' she said, avoiding the issue. 'Have you seen my green blouse?'

'Nope, not sure which one you mean.' Ben's interest had quickly waned. 'Why don't you have some breakfast for a change? They say it's the most important meal of the day.'

'Change the bloody record, I told you I'm not hungry in the mornings. I'll have something when I get to work.'

'Coffee and cake, I bet.'

'My choice.'

Eventually, by 2 pm and after a sandwich, a few cups of coffee and a decongestant tablet, Germaine felt clear headed, if a little queasy. She was aware she was taking more pills than ever in her life and there was a standing joke in the office that her desk drawer was akin to a pharmacist's counter, but she saw that as her only way of keeping going.

She was in the PR meeting with Jeremy and Mark Anderson, and was trying to tell him about the agency's current projects, but she had the distinct impression he was more interested in her cleavage.

'So what do you think, Mark?' she ventured, to test whether he was listening at all.

'Well, there's plenty of scope and a lot of interest in the market at this time. We just need to come up with an interesting angle so we get maximum leverage. In my experience we need to build slowly with this kind of campaign.'

'Why not hit with a big splash?' asked Jeremy. He looked pensive for a change and that threw Germaine a little.

'That would depend on why you want to,' Mark replied. 'Every bit of PR needs to be targeted at achieving both your short-term and your long-term objectives. So if you were aiming to float or sell your company quickly, you might want to issue a lot of releases quickly to build up interest, making people think they'd better act quickly or it might get too expensive. On the other hand, if you want long-term investment and to grow market share, a constant, staggered pattern of releases might be better to indicate stability as well as growth.'

'Am I missing something?' asked Germaine. 'I thought we were talking about raising our profile, but the conversation seems to have changed.'

Mark and Jeremy looked at each other.

'I happen to be meeting a guy from Dunston Capital,' said Jeremy carefully.

'Oh, really?' said Mark, looking suddenly keen. 'I know the UK MD there, Alistair Greenall.'

'That's who I'm meeting,' said Jeremy. 'What are you doing after this? If you're free it might be worth you coming along and we can discuss our plans.'

Germaine felt out of place, if not completely superfluous.

After a moment's hesitation, Jeremy added, 'You too, Germaine, I think it might be useful for you.'

'I've got to do some prep for the Gintech pitch next Monday,' she replied, surprised.

'You've got the weekend,' he answered, giving her a pointed look and then a glance at Mark, who was smiling expectantly.

'I guess we're almost done. Maybe Katherine can run with the rest,' she agreed. 'I'll meet you in reception in five minutes.'

Alistair Greenall was a slightly rotund, well-dressed man in his mid-forties, not what Germaine was expecting. He introduced himself with an awkward handshake and a smile. Mark and he had a bit of friendly banter and Jeremy joined in.

A couple of hours and a few bottles of expensive wine later with only some carrots and celery to soak it up, Germaine was feeling decidedly tipsy, although she was still wondering what she was doing there. The boys were flitting between sports and business conversation, with the odd descent into borderline bawdy humour. The alcohol emboldened Germaine enough to recount stories of her university exploits, which they found hilarious. She was warming to her role, but the boys were drinking heavily and she was struggling to keep up.

Jeremy and Alistair were deep in conversation about Copia and she caught the odd word while pretending to listen to Mark talking about his ex-girlfriend. Then her attention was caught completely when she heard Jeremy say, 'Of course I'm prepared to sell at the right price.'

She could hardly walk properly, but she excused herself and headed to the toilets.

'What the hell, selling the company? Where does that leave me?' she said to herself in the mirror. 'I can't think straight, I need to go.'

She finally managed to extricate herself and, ensconced in the back of a black cab, sleepily checked her phone. She was dismayed to see a number of missed calls from both Sam and Ben, as well as numerous texts. Shit! She'd forgotten about the cinema. It was too late now, it was after 10.

Texting Ben that she'd see him at home, Germaine closed her eyes and let the alcohol muzzle the panic she felt. She dozed, intermittently jerking awake in order to check her progress.

'Here you are, love,' said the taxi driver. 'That's £27. You need a hand?'

'No, I'm OK, thank you,' Germaine mumbled, even though she felt the worse for wear and disoriented.

She clambered out of the cab and fished for her purse in her handbag. After handing over three ten-pound notes, she stumbled into the dark flat and somehow made it to bed. She meant to call Ben, but her phone wasn't to hand so she curled up and dozed off, Jeremy's bombshell about the company's potential sale replaying itself in her mind.

~ 8 ~

Germaine was woken by the sound of someone fumbling at the front door.

'You there?' Ben's slurry voice arrived seconds before his body appeared in the doorway. 'There you are. Where were you?'

'What's the time?' she asked, slumping back on the pillow.

'Don't know. About one.' Ben sat on the bed. 'I kept calling, tried the home number too.'

'You went out afterwards anyway?' Germaine could feel her hackles rising, but was confused about exactly what.

'Well, Sam was in need of a drink and I didn't want to just go home, so yes.' Ben shrugged.

Germaine thought he looked guilty.

'Hold on, you're drunk yourself. So what happened to you?' he said suddenly.

'If you were so concerned, why didn't you come home?'

'Hey, it wasn't me who didn't turn up because I was out getting pissed with work.'

'I don't know where I am with you! You just blow with the wind. You can't be trusted,' said Germaine. What she really wanted to say was that he'd been out with her best friend while she'd been getting messed around by Jeremy, and that she wasn't sure she could trust them.

'What are you talking about?' Ben looked frustrated. 'You're pissed and I can't get any sense out of you. I'm going to sleep in the other room.'

With that he sloped out and she could hear him shifting about the flat.

After a few bouts of Tourettes-like swearing, the alcohol finally drew Germaine down into sleep again.

Even in the cold light of day the following morning, they couldn't come to any happy resolution. Neither would apologise. To Ben it seemed that Germaine was cold and aloof, and Germaine couldn't help feeling that Ben had been unreasonable. If it had been her, she would have come home. She recollected texting the pair that she wouldn't be joining them but she wasn't entirely sure, so she delved in her bag to check. The phone wasn't there.

'Oh no, don't tell me I've lost it. Where on earth's my phone?'

Despite turning the bedroom upside down, there was no sign of it. She got Ben to phone her, but there was no sound of ringing.

'Don't panic, it won't help.' Ben tried to calm her down, but it was like pouring water on burning oil.

'Just bloody help me find it. It's got all my contacts, emails... I can't lose it.'

'It might be here, just out of juice. What did you do when you got in?'

Germaine took a breath and tried to think. 'I don't remember. I think I went straight upstairs for a lie down.'

'Do you recall using the phone in the house?'

'I'm not sure.'

'I got a message from you last night,' said Ben, showing her the text. It had been sent just after ten, so they finally ascertained she must have lost the phone in the cab. Germaine's heart sank at the realisation. How the hell was she going to track down a black cab?

'First things first, call your provider and make sure it's not being used. I'll check the web to see what you do.'

Ben gave her the number to call, and Germaine felt better when she found out her phone hadn't been used. She got the SIM disabled just in case.

'Thanks for your help. I wasn't thinking straight,' she said to Ben, feeling ashamed.

'That's OK, that's what I'm here for,' he said, putting his arm round her.

The panic and anger of the night before had mostly passed, leaving Germaine feeling both relieved and somehow hollow. The best way she could describe it was a solid emptiness from the base of her stomach, pressing up to her heart. She could feel the pulse in her temples, as if the blood was too heavy and struggling to get to the far reaches of her body.

She was exhausted, like she was treading water and in danger of being submerged at any moment. She remembered Theo and the bridge analogy. 'Yep, that's me,' she thought, and it was almost more than she could take.

~ 9 ~

The next couple of weeks were a bit of a blur, with Germaine facing many of the same old problems. She did manage to get her phone back and she struggled through each day without dropping any clangers or having any major issues, but she was so tired all of the time. She concentrated on the mechanics of work – meetings, pitch preparation, client briefs and so on – but continually in the background were the niggling thoughts and feelings about Jeremy and whether he was selling the company, as well as her rocky relationship with Ben.

She remembered what Theo had said about support and on a couple of occasions she did push back on taking on more work, but it didn't seem to make any difference.

'I wouldn't have expected any major changes at this stage, but you're ahead of the game in that you're already aware and have started to put things into practice. It's important to realise that this isn't a quick fix,' said Theo when they met for their first session. 'As I mentioned before, one of the useful areas to explore when you're embarking on this type of journey is feedback, and I've got yours here. I thought it would be beneficial to spend half an hour with you going through the feedback before we start the alignment meeting. Jeremy is going to join us in half an hour. He hasn't seen your feedback and it's entirely up to you whether you want him to.'

Theo pulled a couple of A4 sheets from his bag. 'I will give you this copy, but I want to talk you through it first.'

'I'm a bit nervous, I'm not sure I'll like what I'm going to see,' said Germaine. 'It's funny, because we talk about each other all the time, so I'm not sure what the difference is.'

'Passing comments about people, even to their face, is often more about you, for example "I wish you'd stop talking to me like that",' Theo explained. 'Of course it's useful to tell someone if they're hurting your feelings, but it can also be helpful to share with them how things could be better if they did stop talking to you that way. The feedback we're looking for here has the intention of helping you to improve and that's how you should listen to it.'

'What do you mean, that's how I should listen to it?'

'Let me ask you a question: do you listen differently in different circumstances?'

'Do you mean like sometimes when I talk to my mum or Ben I only half listen and with clients I'm more concentrated?'

'That's an example of a variation in listening, yes,' nodded Theo. 'We vary our listening according to the filters we apply, so in your example your mum and Ben might be talking about something you don't perceive as important, so you stop concentrating. We apply filters to feedback too, so if you believe the people giving you feedback are all stupid, then you're likely to discount anything they say. On the other hand, if you believe that any feedback is potentially useful, you're more likely to examine it and see what truth it holds for you.'

'What you're saying is I should be open-minded about feedback,' said Germaine.

Theo laughed. 'I guess I am. It's information and it's up to you whether you want to use or discard it. It's not *the* truth but it's *their* truth and it's a gift either way. Let me tell you a lovely tale from Buddha's teachings,' he said.

'Buddha was walking into the city market one day and near the city entrance there was a bitter old man sitting on a box. This old man started cursing Buddha, telling him how pretentious he was, how much better he thought he was and how he did nothing worthy of the air he breathed in this world. But Buddha simply smiled and kept on walking to the market to get what he needed.

'The next day Buddha returned to the market and once again the old man was there. This time his cursing intensified, screaming and yelling at Buddha as he walked by, cursing his mother, his father and everyone else in his life. This went on for the rest of the week, until finally as Buddha was leaving the market the man came up to him, his curiosity having simply got the best of him.

'"Buddha, every day you come here smiling, even though every day I curse your name, I curse your family and everything you believe in," the old man said. "And every day you leave through the same entrance with that same smile. I know by speaking to you now that you are not deaf, so why do you keep on smiling while I do nothing but scream the worst things I can think of to your face?"

'The same smile still on his face, Buddha looked at the old man and asked, "If I were to bring you a gift tomorrow morning all wrapped up in a beautiful box, would you accept it?"

'The old man replied, "Absolutely not, I would take nothing from the likes of you!"

'"Aha," Buddha replied. "If I were to offer you this gift and you were to refuse, then who would the gift belong to?"

'"It would still belong to you, of course," answered the old man.

'"And so the same goes with your anger. When I choose not to accept your gift of anger, does it not then remain your own?"'

Germaine found herself with a smile on her face that matched Theo's.

'I'm not saying you should ignore the feedback, but what I am saying is choose which gifts you want to accept,' Theo concluded. 'OK, now to that feedback. I'll share the summary of the three questions and leave you with the detailed report, how does that sound?'

Germaine felt a little anxious, but nodded for him to continue.

'First let's look at what people said were your strengths. The overwhelming impression was that you're dedicated, passionate, inspirational and driven. Your client handling and ability to develop and maintain relationships with your team and clients were universally acknowledged. A couple of people said you're creative and one called you flexible. Another commented on your ability to see the big picture and keep it in mind. How does that strike you?'

Germaine felt a glow of pride and a little embarrassment at hearing what people saw in her. 'I don't know about inspirational and I feel I've been losing my drive,' she said. 'I am a passionate person and I think in general I do show that at work, but again, less so recently.'

'There's a clear theme here of people feeling very engaged by you,' Theo pointed out. 'When something comes so naturally such as your ability to involve others, inspire them and build great relationships, the temptation can be to think that everyone does that and that's definitely not the case. The trick is to be consciously aware of your strengths so you can really leverage them. All the research shows that when you spend the majority of your time using your strengths, you use less energy, which means you can get more done with less stress. It's also more likely to put you into what is called a flow state. This is where you feel like you're in your element and things seem to happen more effortlessly. When times are tough, flow activities provide a sense of purpose and productivity, even though you may be struggling emotionally.'

'OK, what do they say about my weaknesses?' Germaine asked, feeling nervous.

'It's not specifically weaknesses, the question concerns areas for development. The majority of the feedback was about being more balanced, being less defensive, delegating more and asking for help. Half said you need to believe in yourself more and do more strategic thinking. A couple said you need to celebrate your own and others' successes more; a couple that you need to push back a bit more and not be worried by conflict; two also said you need to think more about the company as a whole, not just your team; while one said you need to be more rigorous in the details. How do you feel about that feedback?'

'I guess I kind of expected most of it without really thinking about it. Some of it's fair, but not all of it, and some of it's downright picky.' Germaine could sense herself sitting awkwardly and started to adjust.

'Remember, these comments are gifts,' said Theo. 'You don't have to take them, but don't reject them without looking to see if they might be helpful. Sometimes the hardest message to hear bears the greatest gift. So which one do you have the biggest reaction to?'

'The part about the details, I guess. I know that came from Mike and I suppose he's not wrong – I'm aware it's not a strength of mine, so I should do something about it.'

'What benefits would that bring?' Theo asked matter-of-factly.

'Well, I would feel better prepared when I went into meetings. The one about thinking more about the company sticks in my throat a bit, though, as I think I go beyond the call of duty for the agency.' She could feel a tightness in her throat as she voiced her disappointment.

'Is there any truth in it for you?'

'I guess my first loyalty is to my team. I'm responsible for them, I recruited them and I want to see them thrive. I don't think that's wrong.'

'I can see from the way you're sitting that there's a tension here. You've turned slightly and are twisting away. I'm wondering if that's linked to how you feel about your team and the company, whether you're a bit protective.'

'I guess I am a bit defensive about my team,' Germaine said, thinking of Liam.

'What might be the impact of that defensiveness on other departments?'

'I guess not good – perhaps a little disconnected.'

'Might that sometimes be counter to the good of the company?'

'I see your point, but what do you suggest I do?'

'We'll be looking at that over the course of the coaching, but a good starting point is first to notice how you're feeling and your body posture, then change that to one that's more akin to the state you want to create. For example, stand up now and push your shoulders back.'

Germaine got up and did so, then frowned, aware she had thrust her chest out.

'Not so far,' Theo laughed, 'more subtle – we don't want people thinking you're turning into Barbara Windsor.'

Germaine giggled.

'Just take a deep breath and roll your shoulders back without pushing your chest out. How does that feel?'

'More alert, more open. That's strange. Is it as easy as that?'

'Sometimes, but not always. It all depends on how entrenched you are in a particular state at a given moment.' Theo paused. 'Let's look at the feedback around your impact. I'll read you a couple of individual comments.'

He turned the page and began reading. 'Germaine is an inspiration. She lights up the room when she walks in. She's passionate and very committed to her work. Clients feel like she is on their side, which has been instrumental in the success of the company. She genuinely cares about people and they care about her.'

Germaine was touched. She could feel a welling of pride and warmth. It felt like she'd been seen for who she really was.

'Here's another one,' Theo continued. 'Germaine is one of the main drivers of the business. She's passionate about her job and her team. She pulls out all the stops to get the job done. She leads by example and her team are devoted to her. I wish we could bottle what she has and give some to everyone. It would be even better if she had more self-belief. How does it feel to hear that?'

'It means a lot,' Germaine said softly, not wanting to let her emotions out.

'So there are some great strengths that you need to own and leverage and a few areas to develop. What are you taking from this feedback?'

'That I *am* doing things right, mostly. I need to find some more balance and start to be more strategic as well as working on my self-confidence.'

'What is as clear as a bell is that you have a massive impact on the business. We need to make sure you can continue to do that in a way that sustains both you and the agency,' Theo concluded.

~ 10 ~

Germaine was still trying to get to grips with the feedback when Jeremy arrived for their three-way meeting.

'The purpose of this session is to make sure we're aligned on what we want to achieve from this coaching programme over the next few months,' Theo explained. 'Jeremy, as the sponsor it's your role to make sure those objectives align with those of the business as a whole. Germaine, it's up to you to agree or disagree and to modify the objectives so you feel motivated to achieve them.'

They both nodded.

'First of all, Jeremy, I'd like you to give me a bit of context for the coaching,' Theo continued. 'Can you tell me in your own words why you think coaching might be good for Germaine?'

'Well, we've got some bright, talented people in the business and I've been aware that we're not doing much to develop them.'

'But why Germaine in particular?'

Germaine could feel her cheeks glowing, although she was surprised to see that Jeremy also looked a little uncomfortable.

'OK,' he said to her directly, 'you know you're important to the business and you've done a great job. No one can question your drive and enthusiasm. Your team all love you, though sometimes that's a double-edged sword. You're passionate and you give everything to getting the job done.'

None of this was new, as it was something Jeremy had said on a number of occasions in the pub, but somehow here and now it registered differently to Germaine. She noticed Theo smiling at them both.

'How does it feel hearing that from Jeremy?' he asked her.

'I don't know. It feels really good, but I'm already waiting for the buts.'

'So am I,' said Theo. 'So, Jeremy, what do you want to see more of? What's not working that well here from your perspective?'

'Basically there's nothing wrong, Germaine is great. I just want her to be well and happy. I want her to have more balance and to lighten up a bit and enjoy things.'

Germaine could feel her emotions rapidly shifting from anger to hurt to anger again. 'I know I need more balance, but at the moment chance would be a fine thing!' she thought furiously. Was he looking to sideline her, was that what this coaching was about?

'I'm not sure what balance would look like given that it's a difficult market and we're pretty aggressive on our targets,' she retorted.

'Great question, Germaine, but first I want you to hear what was said. In general people put more emphasis on the negative, so when Jeremy said "you're great, I want you to be happy and enjoy yourself", what you probably heard was "you need more balance and you need to lighten up".'

Theo paused a second for her to absorb this, then continued, 'So what *does* balance look like, Jeremy? How would you know Germaine had it? What things would she be doing differently? How would she be behaving?'

'You would be less defensive about your team, you would get less involved in the detail of the accounts,' Jeremy replied to Germaine. 'You're spreading yourself a bit too thin. I'd like you to be more involved in the strategy for the accounts and the company as a whole.'

Germaine was a little shocked that Jeremy was thinking of her in that way. He'd never spoken to her about it before. She also didn't think she was any good at strategy.

'It would be great to see you stepping back a bit and developing your team, letting them take some of the strain,' he continued. 'Your energy and enthusiasm are vital to this company and I want you to have more of an active role in driving it forward, but at the moment you're overloaded and you need to find a way to delegate more. Sometimes when you come in you look shattered and people are concerned about you.'

'How does that feel to you, Germaine?' asked Theo.

Germaine was a bit concerned, but she tried not to show it. 'I guess I do put a lot of pressure on myself,' she said slowly.

'What's the result of carrying that additional pressure?' asked Theo.

'I get so tired and I take so many things quite personally, as I feel very responsible.'

'What else?'

'I guess others end up being distanced from some of the pressure, but if they're going to move upwards then they need to know what it's like and be able to handle it.'

Theo nodded in agreement and turned to Jeremy. 'What else would you like to see more of from Germaine?'

'Probably a bit more belief in herself. Don't get me wrong,' he said, turning to look at Germaine, 'it's not like you're lacking in confidence, it's just that I would like to see you holding your own a bit more and pushing back, especially to the likes of Mike.'

'What benefits would that bring?' probed Theo.

'Well, you're pretty intuitive and sometimes see things that the rest of us don't. But we're a fairly headstrong bunch, so you need to be prepared to fight your corner and that can be uncomfortable. If you don't, I think we may be missing out on some good opportunities with our people and as a business.'

'So let's get clear,' said Theo, 'the objectives of the coaching could be...' While he was talking he was writing on a sheet of paper. 'First, developing your strategic thinking capabilities. That means creating the time to focus on company-wide initiatives and more active delegation to the next level down.

'Second,' he continued, 'creating more balance in work and in life. That means looking after yourself and ensuring that the tank gets regularly refuelled. And third, developing more leadership gravitas and self-belief. That means building on your level of self-confidence so that you feel less knocked off centre and more able to hold your ground with others at a senior level.'

Germaine and Jeremy both nodded in agreement.

'That sounds good and it looks like we're all clear on the areas that need addressing,' said Jeremy.

'Yes, I think we are and it feels do-able,' added Germaine, who was looking forward to the next steps.

~ 11 ~

By the time she was due to meet Theo for their first coaching session, the pressures of the job had reversed Germaine's mood once again. That morning she'd got dressed in a hurry and wasn't sure the shoes she was wearing went with her trousers – and she could see an iron mark on those. She'd hastily eaten half a sandwich for lunch, taken at her desk. 'I'm really not ready,' she thought.

'So, how have things been since I last saw you?' asked Theo when they'd sat down.

'I'm going to be straight with you, I feel exhausted and I'm not sure I have the energy for this.'

'This as in the coaching session, coaching in general or life as a whole?' Theo smiled.

'You think I'm being melodramatic, don't you?'

'Just in need of some support,' he said. 'So you're exhausted and overloaded. How does that make you feel?'

'Right now, bloody awful!' Germaine had the familiar sensation of her chest being clamped and her throat squeezed. She choked back the tears that had started to break free, but she couldn't stop them.

'It's OK to cry,' Theo said.

After a few moments she heaved a sigh, took the tissues Theo offered her and said, 'Sorry about this, I don't know what's got into me.'

'Do you mind if I try something?' he said, moving a little closer.

'What?'

'It's called the emotional freedom technique or EFT. It involves lightly tapping points on your face and hands while you bring up thoughts that you have an emotional reaction to. These points are called energy meridians. They've been used for centuries in Chinese medicine, for things like acupuncture. By tapping on them you balance your energy system. You see, our subconscious is what's controlling our emotional state most of the time – we think it's all happening on a conscious level, but in reality our subconscious is running the show. What we feel about something is stored in our bodies, in our energy system. If we can give the energy system a clear slate when bringing up these 'charged' thoughts, they stop having a hold over us. This technique is a way of accessing the subconscious directly, which is what makes it really powerful. Are you game?'

'Er, OK.'

'How do you feel right now?'

'Exhausted, sad.' Germaine could feel the tears coming again.

'Repeat after me, "Even though I feel exhausted and sad, I deeply and completely accept myself."'

As Germaine repeated the sentence, Theo started to lightly tap points on her face and then her hands. After she had said the sentence a couple of times, he stopped, looked at her and asked, 'On a scale of 1 to 10, with 1 being not at all and 10 being extremely, how exhausted and sad do you feel right now?'

'Right now, a lot less than a minute ago – maybe a 7?'

'Great, let's do it again. This time you tap on yourself and follow me.'

They repeated the exercise and when asked again to score how she felt, Germaine said, 'That's weird. I don't feel sad now, although I still feel exhausted.' She could hear how dull her voice sounded.

'At a guess you've been under stress for a while now and it's only natural you're exhausted,' said Theo. 'Part of the coaching process will be getting you to be aware of your energy and how to manage it, from a physical, emotional and mental perspective. So how do you feel about your life and work right now?'

'I think I might have to quit, but I can't.'

'And how does that feel?'

'Like shit. I'm trapped. I want to succeed and prove I can do it... I can't afford to lose everything I've achieved. Other people seem to manage to do it, why the hell can't I? What's wrong with me?' Tears were running down Germaine's cheeks again.

Theo supplied her with another tissue, which she took and blew her nose unselfconsciously.

'So you're feeling trapped, you're afraid of losing what you've created and you feel you ought to be able to do this because others can.'

'It sounds so weak and stupid...'

'And?'

'That's not me. I get things done. I'm a positive person.'

'So what's the fear?'

'That I'm weak.'

'What else?'

'That I'm silly.'

'So you're scared that you're weak and silly. How does that feel?'

'Not good – it's sapping.' With that Germaine let out a sigh and looked Theo in the eye. 'I'm tired of it. It shouldn't be this way.'

'Ignoring the shoulds and shouldn'ts for now, how do you *want* to feel?'

'Good about myself, what I'm doing, secure, full of energy.'

'How much do you think it's possible for you to feel that way?'

'At the moment, not at all.'

'Not at all? Have you ever felt that way at work?'

'I guess so, but I can't remember when.'

Theo got up and went to the window. 'Come over here.'

When Germaine joined him, facing the window, he smiled and asked her, 'When was the last time you felt energised at work?'

After a few seconds she replied, 'Umm, last year, I think.'

An image of herself came into her mind, tanned and breezing into the office having secured the second largest contract in their history the day before. She smiled.

'Aha, there you go. What's going on right now?'

'I'm remembering the buzz in the office. We'd just won a great contract. It was pretty significant in that it meant we could diversify and grow the business. It was a prestigious client and you could tell everyone was happy – me too. All our hard work had paid off and we knew we would do a great job. It just felt right.'

'Your face has lit up. How are you feeling right now?'

'Now?' Germaine paused and frowned. 'Tired.'

'You just jumped back to before your story. How did you feel while you were thinking of the time you were energised?'

'Happy, I guess, but that was then. I can't go around thinking about the past.'

'Interesting. What do you notice about your feelings and energy state from that exercise?'

'I don't know. My feelings seem to be linked with what I'm thinking about, and my energy too. I guess it's obvious, but I don't think I ever made the connection before.'

'That's a profound realisation and worthy of exploration' said Theo, smiling. 'On that note, I've got a gift for you.'

He handed her a leather-bound book. 'This is a journal. I want you to write down any insights you have or important things you learn, plus I'll be asking you to do a number of exercises that you'll need this for. Now, read me what you see on the first page.'

She opened the book and started to read. 'Between stimulus and response there is a space. In that space is our power to choose our response. In our response lies our growth and our freedom.' There was a little illustration of a butterfly next to the quote, which she could see was from Viktor Frankl.

'Write the date and then this question,' Theo continued. '"What makes me lose energy?" That will be part of your homework between sessions, to answer that question. Don't worry if it's well written or even makes sense, just write your thoughts as they come. And as part of becoming aware of how and when you become overloaded, I'd like you to start observing and recording what you eat and drink and how you feel in the morning, afternoon and evening.'

Germaine was silent, wondering how she was supposed to do all this and her job as well.

'It may seem like a lot of work,' said Theo, almost as if he was reading her mind. 'But it's just a few minutes here and there. And what's the alternative, to keep doing what you're doing? I think you know where that will lead you in the end.'

Germaine could only nod.

'Doing this is vital because it begins the journey of becoming conscious of your thoughts and actions and their consequences, and you'll also be taking action to move yourself out of a place where you feel helpless and disempowered. Are you prepared to commit to that?'

'I guess so.'

'Don't say yes to please me.'

Germaine was taken aback. It was his idea, why was he challenging her?

Theo continued, 'This is the start of the rest of your life. If you're going to commit, make sure you do so because you want to. So why would you want to, for the sake of what?'

Germaine could feel her heartbeat pick up and she felt suddenly exposed. This was all a bit more real somehow. 'Because I don't want to feel this way,' she said slowly.

'And why's that?'

'Because it's killing me.'

'So for the sake of being alive – sounds pretty damned important, doesn't it?'

She nodded.

Theo beamed. 'OK, will you write this down: "I commit to observing and recording when and what I eat and drink and how I feel in the morning, afternoon and evening." If you think this is going to be hard to remember, you could create reminder appointments on your phone or computer. Now, I think we need a break and a cup of tea – that can be the first thing you write down!'

~ 12 ~

When they restarted the session after the break, Theo said, 'I'd like to do a bit more exploration of where you are now so we can check on our progress throughout the programme. There's a tool we use for this purpose called the wheel of life, which you'll find at the back of your journal.'

Germaine flicked through the pages and saw some diagrams that looked like targets, complete with concentric circles numbered 1 to 10. The targets were divided into segments, with labels such as health, money, fun/leisure and spirituality.

'If 1 is as low as it can be and 10 is couldn't be better in terms of your levels of satisfaction, what I'd like you to do is draw a line in each section that indicates where you are now. For example, for money you might say a 7, because you're pretty comfortable. This isn't set in stone, it's just a snapshot in time. Is that clear?'

'Yes, I think so,' replied Germaine.

'OK. Can you spend a few minutes marking where you are now for each sector?'

Germaine started to fill out the wheel, but then stopped and asked, 'What do you mean by spirituality? I'm not religious at all, if that's what you're referring to.'

'Spirituality is the dimension of your life that feels connected to some greater meaning or purpose. It's your wheel, you can choose what has most significance for you. So it could mean feeling fulfilled or even doing spiritual practices such as meditation, yoga or reading stuff that develops you as an individual. Another way to think about it is the connection you might make with your inner world of thoughts, emotions, awareness, beliefs and how that links up with your outer world.'

At some level this resonated for Germaine, but she had never really made the connection, at least consciously. 'Could I say all of that?' she asked.

'Sure, as long as you know what you mean.'

Having filled out her wheel Germaine felt a little non-plussed. She'd known instinctively what was happening, but seeing it in black and white in front of her made it somehow more real. Her health and her life outside of her job were paying the price for her being successful and making good money at work.

'Which section stands out for you?' asked Theo.

'Health – I gave that and fun/leisure a 3.'

'What does a 3 look like to you?'

Germaine could feel emotion bubbling to the surface. 'Like I said before, I'm tired a lot of the time. I even fell asleep at the hairdressers the other day while my hair was being cut! I'm getting headaches and I'm aware I'm popping too many pills. I know that when it comes to winter I'm going to get everything that's going around the office.'

Theo nodded, but said nothing.

'I used to do lots of classes and go running and biking at the weekend,' she continued. 'Now it's a miracle if I get to the gym once a week. I know it's down to me, but...'

'I can hear your frustration. What's holding you back?'

'Not having time! I've got too much work to do and I don't have the energy. I feel like a hamster on a wheel.'

'That sounds like a pretty clear perspective: I don't have time to be healthy.'

'When you say it like that it sounds silly,' said Germaine, her cheeks flushing.

'But would you say that's the perspective you hold?'

'I guess so.'

'And it's leaving you feeling tired and lacking in energy?'

Germaine nodded. She felt tired just thinking about it.

'Any other feelings coming up?'

'Hopelessness.'

'So tired, lacking in energy and feeling hopeless. What possibilities are there for you here?'

'None. Well, I could quit my job, but I don't want to do that.' Germaine felt a slight wave of panic – was that what Theo was leading her to?

'So that's the "No time to be healthy" perspective, is there another one?'

'It's up to me to be healthy?'

'Interesting. Did you notice that the last perspective started with 'it's down to me'? You're saying the same but with a different energy.'

'"Down to me" feels like the burden of responsibility is on me, whereas "up to me" sounds like I have a choice.'

'Brilliant, exactly so. Let's move to the other end of the table.'

Having done so, Theo continued, 'So what's the "It's up to me" perspective like?'

'I can choose to do things that are healthy when the opportunity presents itself.'

'Such as?'

'Stop eating cakes when they're offered to me.'

'And?'

'Stop drinking so much, stop finishing the bottle because it's open.'

'And?'

'Stop having those "social" cigarettes.'

'I'm noticing a pattern here, are you?'

'That I've got a lot of bad habits? I'm no nun.'

Theo laughed. 'Not that specifically. I thought you might want to rename the perspective "I'll be healthy when I stop". How does that make you feel?'

'Naughty, and a bit anxious.'

'I'm getting an image of you as a teenager rebelling against her parents.'

Germaine's stomach tightened.

'Where did you go just then?' asked Theo, noticing her expression.

'Not sure what you mean... I'm still here.'

She felt as if Theo was evaluating her with a kind of detached empathy, like he was calculating the best path for his questions.

'What are you feeling right now?' he asked after a short pause.

'A bit of anger.'

'So the "I'll be healthy when I stop" perspective makes you feel naughty, anxious and a bit angry. What are the possibilities here?'

'I'm not sure. I'm not even sure I believe that stopping all of these things will make me healthy.'

'OK, but what might you be able to do if you did stop?'

'I guess I'd need less exercise because I wouldn't be eating so many calories, and I might have more energy because my body wouldn't be working so hard getting rid of toxins. More energy would mean I might be able to do more of the things I want to outside of work.'

'Great. Now let's go back to the "It's up to me" perspective. There's a big part of that that is "I get to choose". Do you follow me?'

Germaine nodded.

'You're the centre of it all. It really is all up to you and it always has been. Where should we go for this perspective?

Be as silly or audacious as you like, I'm right there with you.'

The gleam in Theo's eyes was challenging the dare-devil in her. 'Right, you asked for it,' she thought, climbing on the table. Theo chuckled and followed her.

Now that she was up there she felt a bit exposed, but seeing Theo beaming back at her gave her the feeling of being a kid again.

'How does this feel?' he asked.

'A bit scary, a bit exposed, but exhilarating and free, like anything's possible.'

'So in terms of health, what's possible from here?'

'If I feel like going for a bike ride, I will. If I want to go climbing at the weekend, I can. And yoga's going to be part of my daily routine.'

She thought for a while then added, 'You know, being here makes me realise that my health isn't second place but primary. Ignoring it's not an issue.'

'My health is primary – that's one for the journal. Say it out loud again.'

'My health is primary.'

'How does it feel, saying that?'

'Great.'

'You look radiant. Breathe that feeling in, remember it. Is there a word that represents this feeling for you?'

'Vibrant works, I think.'

'OK, so this is the vibrant you. And being the vibrant you, what does daily yoga look like?'

'Realistically I can't do a class every day.'

'So what would a typical day in the life of the vibrant you look like?'

After a few minutes, Germaine said, 'I would wake up, do some yoga stretches, have a light breakfast, get to work early. Drink mostly water at work. Go for a walk at lunchtime and perhaps eat surrounded by a bit of greenery. Make sure I eat some fruit in the afternoon and get home early so I can go to a class at least three nights a week. Drink less wine.'

'What about a weekly colonic irrigation and a course in Zen meditation thrown in for good measure?' Theo looked at her straight-faced.

She burst out laughing and he joined in.

'I get that you're passionate and enthusiastic,' he continued. 'It's a common pattern to take on a lot and then beat yourself up when you don't do everything. So excluding the colonics, are there one or two things that stand out for you?'

'Drinking less wine and exercising.'

'As they say, Rome wasn't built in a day, and old habits die hard. It's also said that a new habit takes 30 days to stick. How important is it to you to feel like the vibrant you?'

'Very.'

'And do you think doing these things will help you get to the vibrant you?'

'Well, they won't do any harm. I might even be able to wear my favourite bikini again this summer.'

She felt a little nervous at the idea of committing to doing these things for 30 days, but it did feel important at that moment.

'Remember, you can set up calendar reminders to prompt you, and use friends and colleagues to help keep you on the path. Plus of course you'll be writing everything in your journal,' said Theo, smiling.

'Yes, I think I'll need Ben to help me on the wine front, and I'll check out the evening exercise classes when I get back to my desk.'

~ 13 ~

Germaine got home early for a change. 'This is nice,' she thought, as they sat down to a microwave dinner for two and a glass of wine.

Ben and she chatted about their respective days, then he fetched his laptop. 'Sorry, just got a few emails to send tonight,' he explained as he put the computer on the table. 'That OK?'

'Of course. I'll just read for a change.' She went into the living room and noticed her bag by the door, the corner of her new journal poking out.

'I guess I should do my homework,' she thought, but noticed her resistance. She wanted to put the journal down almost as soon as she'd picked it up, and was about to do so when Ben came through the door.

'I've poured you another glass, do you want anything else?'

'No, I'm good,' she said. 'No excuses, Germaine,' she told herself.

Ben wandered back to the kitchen, where he was obviously engrossed in something on his laptop. Germaine opened her journal and stared at the butterfly at the top of the first page. Its wings were slightly apart, as if preparing to flutter into the air. She remembered her commitments and looked at the wine.

She read the question again: 'What makes me lose energy?'

'I don't really know,' she thought.

She could hear Ben chatting on the phone and laughing.

'What the hell am I doing this for?' she thought and started to put the journal down. Then she caught herself.

'I lose energy when someone pisses me off,' she wrote. 'Like Ben.'

'Who else pisses me off?' she thought, and added, 'Jeremy and Mike when they go off in their huddles. That twat down the road who lets his dog shit on our path.'

She could feel her indignation rising.

'And taxi drivers who moan at you or rip you off.'

She was getting into this and quite enjoying venting. After a page and a half some of the entries had become funny to her and she burst out laughing. 'What a grumpy old woman I am,' she thought. 'I wonder if he'd notice if I tore out the page?'

'ANGER AND RESENTMENT SAP MY ENERGY' she wrote and underlined it.

She thought about the night she lost her phone and the bombshell of Jeremy looking to sell the company. The anger and resentment came back, not as strong as at the time, but still enough to make her want to put down the journal. She took a swig of wine and tried to think of something else.

Mulling over her day at work, she remembered a conversation with Mike about her pension plan. She had felt embarrassed at the time and still did recalling it. Financial stuff was all gobbledegook to her. She'd seen the disdain in Mike's face when she'd asked a simple question or hadn't grasped a point.

She picked up her journal and wrote: 'Being crap at numbers and being made to feel small.'

She recognised that as the feeling she sometimes had at board meetings – as if her opinion was less important or valid and she was in danger of embarrassing herself if she ventured outside her expertise. She added: 'Not being myself with the board members – second guessing myself.'

Then Germaine remembered she was also supposed to be writing down what she ate, drank and did and how she felt during the day – and that she hadn't done it. How typical. She added to her list of energy drainers: 'Not doing what I said I would because I don't have the time.'

She stared at her entries, looked at her wine and wrote 'drinking too much wine' – then she drained the glass.

Returning to the page, she supposed that should be under a separate heading, so she crossed out the line, turned to a new page, put the date and wrote 'Activity Diary' across the top, then 'Morning' underneath.

She could almost hear Ben's voice saying 'No breakfast again' and grumbled to herself. Then she wrote:

- 2 coffees and a piece of shortbread
- Glass of water
- 2 hours of meetings, 1½ hours at desk
- Pension meeting with Mike. Felt a bit zapped.
- Lunch – BLT sandwich at desk. 2 cups of coffee and a sneaky fag.
- Throat lozenge due to a tickly throat.
- 3 hours of meetings, 2 hours at desk. Coaching meeting.
- Glass of water
- Tired but OK
- Dinner – microwave curry with Ben and 1½ glasses of wine. Journaling, feeling a bit angry and resentful.

She tried to think of when she felt really full of energy. She realised she was looking at one of Ben's magazines with a mountain bike in full flight. She wrote down:

- Exercising, riding a bike, dancing, classes, yoga, walking in nature, animals

What about at work?

- Seeing my team develop, helping drive the company forward

She was on a roll.

Just then, Ben popped his head round the door. 'Hey, Ger, guess what? Some of the guys are going off to climb Kilimanjaro next November. Mark's going to come from San Francisco. It would be great to do it and catch up with Mark. What d'ya think?' Not waiting for a response, he went back to his conversation.

Mark was a university friend of Ben's. He was in advertising too, but had been fast tracked and was now heading up his own agency in San Francisco. He was married with two kids and had a fabulous house and what seemed to be the perfect life. Germaine had got on really well with his wife Jerry, but she couldn't help feeling a bit envious of the two of them.

She flipped back to the first page of the journal and added to the 'Where do I lose energy?' list: 'Comparing myself to others and not matching up'.

With that, she flicked on the television and started to watch *Big Brother*, something she hadn't done for years. Fifteen minutes later her mind had wandered and she could feel herself slouching into the sofa.

'What am I doing?' she thought. She picked up the journal again and wrote, 'Watching dross on TV'.

'I haven't read a book in ages,' she thought. 'Where's that new one Sam gave me?'

~ 14 ~

As Germaine climbed into the leather bucket seat of the Audi TT hire car, she realised it was an automatic. She had never driven an automatic car and contemplated going back into the rental office to get an exchange. But time was ticking and she hadn't allowed much room for complications.

'It can't be that hard,' she thought. 'I'll give it a go.'

She turned the key and released the handbrake, moving the gearstick to drive and putting her foot on the accelerator. The car lurched forward. She slammed on the brake, prompting some curious looks from passing pedestrians.

Adjusting to the sensitivity of the car, she moved forward gently and turned onto the main road. Things were looking up: the car had a sporty feel to it. But her approach to the first set of traffic lights broke the spell, the car kangarooing along the road for 10 metres when she put her foot on the brake.

'What the hell is going on?' she shouted.

Trying to keep calm she managed to pull off smoothly from the lights, but she still had problems every time she needed to stop. By the time she reached work she was on the verge of tears.

Dumping her bag, she headed straight to the kitchen for a coffee. Tom crossed the office to join her.

'What's up, Germaine?'

'Bloody hire car,' she snapped. 'It's a nightmare to drive. I'm supposed to be doing a coaching session in 15 minutes and there are things I needed to get done before the session that I haven't. Arrgggghhh!'

'What kind of car?' he asked.

'TT automatic. Looks great, but it's uncontrollable.'

'Have you driven an automatic before?'

'Nope, but isn't it supposed to be easier?'

'I bet you're using both feet at the same time. That's what you do naturally and that's what I did. The trick is only to use one leg to drive with and keep the other out of the way.'

Germaine felt herself flush with embarrassment. 'I think you're right. How stupid of me.'

She was still worked up when Theo arrived for another session.

'What's wrong?' he asked after they'd sat down.

'Just some crap with my car, nothing really. The thing is, I'd been feeling generally better and I'd been doing the things I'd committed to. It's typical of me, I start something and get waylaid somehow.'

'What happened that you found challenging?' he asked, smiling.

'My car is in the garage and I needed a hire car, so I got this little TT. It looks great, but it's an automatic and I've never driven one before. I should have gone back to change it, but I didn't have time. It was hopping all over the place and I felt really stupid.'

'So what can you learn from that?'

'Umm, I guess there's a bunch of stuff. I should have said I didn't want an automatic car, which means I should have been clear about my requirements.'

'Anything else?'

'I didn't have time to change the car because I was late, so maybe I need to give myself more time. And getting upset and stressed about the situation only seemed to make it worse. This kind of thing happens all the time to me.'

'Good. Can you see how this event might be a metaphor for you right now?' Theo asked.

Thinking again about what Tom had said, she offered, 'When I'm in a new situation, my old behaviours don't guarantee success and can actually be counter-productive.'

'Brilliant! We mostly operate on automatic, using our normal coping strategies and habits, so when we're in a new environment and they don't work as expected, we get anxious. It's just the same if we commit ourselves to doing something new: the world and our beliefs make us resistant. So how do you feel now?'

'A bit better, but I'm not sure why.'

'Well, partly it's because when you try to get above something to see what you can learn from it, you make it less personal. It's important for you to be aware of that as a leader, because if you feel uneasy about something that happened in a different context, people in your team will experience that unease, even if they don't know what caused it.'

'But what can I do about that? I can't be in control all the time.'

'There are different strategies depending on the situation. Think about what parents do. If a child were pushing your buttons and you felt yourself getting wound up, you could count to ten before reacting. That can work just as well with adults.' Theo smiled. 'Anyway, how did your homework go? What did you notice from filling in your journal?'

'Well, the first thing I noticed was that I stopped drinking as much coffee, just by the fact I knew I was going to be writing it down later. I had water instead. I also realised that the vast majority of the food I eat is pre-packed, whether that's sandwiches for lunch or a microwave dinner. But there's another side to it as well.'

'What's that?' prodded Theo.

'I've been avoiding certain people, for example the guys at Dixies. I know that if I go in there I'll end up drinking coffee and coming out with an armful of cakes, and I even walked past Stefano, the owner, the other day and pretended I hadn't seen him. I felt so guilty.'

'So the habit is going into Dixies and accepting cakes and coffee whether it's what you really want or not, and that's keeping you in the pattern of behaviour that you're trying to change.'

'Yep, that sounds about right.'

'What could the belief be that's stopping you from breaking that habit?'

Germaine thought for a while. 'That they'll be offended if I refuse?'

'And what's behind that? If they were offended, what would that make you feel about yourself?'

'That they won't like me any more?'

'Good – and behind that?'

Germaine's throat was dry and the words stuck in her mouth. 'That they would reject me...'

'And what if they did reject you?' Theo asked gently.

'I'd lose that feeling of being special. They're such a sweet bunch and they're so lovely to me.'

Germaine could feel the tears welling up. Theo passed her a tissue. 'So what's behind that?'

She opened her mouth to speak, but the words wouldn't come at first. She swallowed and finally said, 'That I don't deserve them, that I'm not good enough.'

She had a flash of an obscure memory from when she was a little girl, but it was gone before she could make sense of it. After a minute or so, she stopped crying and let out an involuntary sigh.

Theo seemed to use that as a prompt. 'Our beliefs can live deep within us and until we shine a light on them they run the show, creating habits, behaviours and unexplained emotions. My guess is you know logically you *are* good enough, but deep down something happened that made you tell yourself you're not. There are several ways of dealing with these subconscious beliefs. For now, I think using the emotional freedom technique I showed you before would be great.'

Germaine nodded, not confident in her voice to speak aloud.

'OK, let's start with the clearing. Rubbing here, say out loud: "Even though I feel I'm not good enough, I completely and deeply love and accept myself."'

They worked through the tapping points until Germaine felt neutral about the statement, then did the process again but this time repeating the phrase 'I am enough'. At the end of three rounds, Germaine said, 'I feel somehow more grounded and solid, but in a good way.'

They both laughed.

'So looking at the situation at Dixies, let's think about what you really want,' said Theo. He started to count on his fingers. 'First, to be able to choose what you want to eat and drink, right?'

'Yep, without feeling guilty.'

'And?'

'To keep the easy relationship I have with them.'

'OK, let's play a little game. You take on the role of Stefano and I'll be you. First let's go to the current situation. What's happening at the moment?'

'When I go past I'd normally glance in and wave if there was someone there or even pop in and get a coffee. But at the moment I'm rushing by, pretending I'm really late.'

'OK, you're Stefano, get into his body, his mannerisms and so on.'

Germaine plumped herself up a little and swaggered around, chuckling at herself.

Theo nodded and took on her own persona. He played with his hair and mimicked her facial expressions so successfully that she was taken aback.

She tried to get into her role, clearing and cleaning with a tea towel as she pictured Stefano doing, with an open smile as he saw Germaine passing the window. Theo walked briskly past in front of her, not looking at her.

'OK,' he said. 'How did you feel as Stefano?'

'Strangely, not what I expected. I was aware something was up and I was being avoided, but I was just curious. I expected to feel a bit hurt.'

'That's interesting. I felt a little angry at him and a lot at myself,' Theo observed.

'You're right, I did feel a bit angry – at myself for feeling guilty and at him for making me so.'

'So how do you think you would behave if you had what you wanted?'

'I guess I'd be firm, but also matter-of-fact about what I wanted. More honest, I guess. It's a bit scary, though.'

'But what's the worst that could happen?'

'That they did reject me and I became just another customer. That would be a shame, but I'd survive.'

'And what's the best that could happen?'

'I feel silly saying it, but that I could be honest and true to myself and not dent the relationship. Is it that simple?'

'Does this pattern show up anywhere else in your life – at work, for example?'

Germaine laughed. 'Everywhere! When I deal with the board I'm scared of saying something stupid, so I hold myself back. It's the same with my team, but to a lesser extent. I have to show them that I'm on top of things and lead by example by working long hours and with a passion, even when I'm sapped of energy. With Ben I hold back what I feel because I don't want to seem needy or weak, but the feeling builds until it gets too big and then it comes out in an ugly way.'

'It sounds like a great pattern to bust, then.' Theo smiled. 'But let's get back to Stefano and Dixies. What action are you going to take?'

'I think I'll pop in this afternoon and have a juice. If he asks me if I want a cake, I'll tell him I'm on a programme and have to say no.'

'And what about the feeling of being special, is there a way of keeping that?'

'I don't know.'

'OK, let's leave that as an open question. Can you write that down in your journal?'

Germaine went to where she'd entered that morning's food and energy diary, and turned over a new page. There at the top was a drawing of an ant on a crumpled leaf. She read the quote next to it to herself: 'In the absence of clearly defined goals, we become strangely loyal to performing daily trivia until ultimately we become enslaved by it.'

Thinking that was quite apt, she wrote out her question.

'Right, so shall we return to the board or your team?' Theo asked.

'The team,' Germaine piped up, a little too quickly for her own liking.

Theo smiled, but didn't take the bait. 'If I remember correctly, you feel you have to show them that you're in control and set them an example by working long hours. Tell me a bit more about that.'

'I have a great team and a great relationship with them. We're meeting all our targets.'

'I hear a *but*.'

'It's the same old – it just feels too much sometimes.'

'What would happen if you didn't work such long hours? What would you be role modelling?'

'Well, I couldn't do as much, but I'd be role modelling that work isn't everything, that it's OK to have a life as well.'

'And what do you believe would happen to the results?'

'That they'd suffer.'

'What evidence do you have for that?'

'It's obvious, isn't it? You get out what you put in.'

'Interesting. So in your equation you put in hard work and you get out hard work. What would you like to get out instead?'

Germaine laughed. 'I want the team to feel excited when coming to work, to feel engaged, stimulated, passionate and also to produce great results.'

'Great, can you write that in your journal?'

He waited for Germaine to finish writing, then continued, 'So do you put excitement, engagement, stimulation and passion into your work at the moment?'

'Not really, I've lost my mojo.'

'Maybe this is a good place to look at the rest of your homework, about energy drains and producers. What did you write about energy producers?'

'Going for walks, cycling along the river, having a laugh with friends. And at work, developing my team and bringing in the results that help drive the company forward.'

'So you've started to look at the things that give you energy,' said Theo, 'I want you to build on that list by looking at things that you loved to do growing up. Then consider what stops you doing those things now and explore the beliefs behind that. We tend not to question our beliefs as we think that's just the way things are.'

'What do you mean?' asked Germaine.

'Let me give you an example. I worked with a client last year who believed that he wasn't good with people and that this would hold him back from furthering his career. From a young age he was told that he was a loner and a bit shy, and as a result he never felt that relaxed around others. By becoming aware of this belief, he realised he actually had a choice about what he believed about himself.'

'So you mean I should think about what I believe about myself that's draining my energy?'

'Yes, and keep doing your eating and energy diary – it's a way of monitoring how you're progressing. And one more thing, tap in "I am worthy" in the way we did earlier, every night and morning. If any other emotion pops up, do the same: "Even though I feel (whatever it is), I deeply love and accept myself".'

'OK, I think I can cope with that,' Germaine agreed, and smiled.

'There's another process that might be useful, called "The Journey",' Theo said. 'A friend of mine can help you with that – here are her details.' He scribbled on one of his cards and gave it to her. Germaine thanked him and put the card in her purse, scarcely registering it beyond the name Susan Watts.

~ 15 ~

After the session Germaine felt lighter and more energised.

'What's happened?' asked Tom when he saw her. 'You look younger all of a sudden. You've not gone and had that botox, have you?'

'As if.' Germaine fought the urge to go and check herself in the bathroom mirror. 'I'd like to say I'd found a miracle anti-ageing cream, but I'd be lying.'

'Let's grab a coffee. I'm curious to hear about your sessions with Theo.'

They headed to the office kitchen. Tom collected two cups. 'The usual?'

'Actually, you know what, I think I'll have a peppermint tea.'

'Did he tell you to give up coffee?'

'No, I don't really fancy it,' said Germaine. 'I'd rather have a proper one down at Dixies later. Theo does have me looking at what I eat and drink, though, and what has an effect on my energy.'

'Sounds more like a nutritionist.' Tom looked disappointed.

'Well, that's a small part of it. I also look at my life and work and how fulfilled I am in the different aspects of that.'

'Like you work too hard and don't have any balance?'

Germaine laughed. 'You know me too well.'

'It sounds obvious stuff, but something's having an effect. You seem more how you used to be. It's really nice to see.' Tom looked genuinely pleased and Germaine felt quite touched.

Later that afternoon after a couple of back-to-back meetings, she was sitting at her desk. Most of her team were there, looking busy and engaged in what they were doing. They also seemed to be a bit more peaceful, as if they were mirroring how she felt. Now that was a strange thought.

Katherine looked up and smiled. 'How's it going with the coaching, or shouldn't I ask?'

'It's going well, as far as I can tell.'

'I wanted to pass by you some ideas I had for our campaign, when you've got time. I also had a thought about doing an internal event to widen the creative pool.'

'Shit, how does she have the time?' thought Germaine, then said out loud, 'That's great. Right now OK?'

Katherine went off to find a meeting room, and Germaine realised she'd just had an emotional trigger. What had Theo said? What was the pattern? When someone in her team did something better than she could have done, she felt threatened. So what was the belief? That they were better than her?

She picked up her journal and scribbled down, 'Katherine, great idea, challenges me, feel threatened, better than me?'

Just writing the entry made her feel better, she realised.

Katherine was brimming with enthusiasm at their meeting. Germaine took some of her campaign ideas and made some slight tweaks, and they both agreed they had a fabulous proposition that they could run by creative and planning the following day.

Back at her desk, Germaine wondered again about her journal entry. She looked in her diary for what she'd said she wanted from her team: excitement, engagement, stimulation and passion. A light bulb went on in her head.

She realised that was only part of it – she also wanted ease and playfulness and a sense of working together for a common purpose.

Analysing it a little more, the feeling was fear of being undermined, usurped and overshadowed; and the habit was to want to exert control and dampen things down. That was at odds with wanting her team to be engaged and feel empowered; no wonder she felt tense about it. So what had worked this time?

She wrote in her journal: 'Changing how I felt, by writing it down, enabled me to just be with the possibilities and brainstorm.'

'I sound all new-agey,' she thought. 'I'll be on the wheatgrass juice next.'

She looked around to check that no one had noticed her embarrassed laugh.

~ 16 ~

Ben was away for a couple of nights, sorting a few things out for his dad in Nottingham. Normally Germaine would have got a bit irked, but now she felt herself looking forward to some time on her own with no distractions. Tom had loaned her a leadership book he said he had partially read and found enlightening, and she thought she might give that a go tonight.

First things first, she reached for her journal. After doing her food, drink and energy diary, she paused. 'Let me have a look at what's happened up to now,' she thought. 'I wonder if there's been much of a change apart from drinking less coffee and a little less wine? I've been to a couple of classes, but it's not really enough.'

Reading the start of the journal, she was struck by how consistently she felt anxious and foggy-headed at the start of the day, wired at lunchtime and exhausted by the time she got home. Her coffee consumption and sugar intake had dropped, she knew, even from the beginning of the programme, but the headaches and sinus problems hadn't stopped. That was still a problem she was concerned about.

After reading through all her entries she started to see other changes. They weren't things she'd explicitly set out to do, yet she could see they'd emerged from the commitment and focus she had on her health. She also noted that she'd started taking more breaks and that had coincided with a reduction in the number of times she felt exhausted.

'I need to do my homework,' she thought. 'What were the questions?' She looked at what she'd written:

- Is there a way of allowing Stefano to feel like he's taking care of me that also works for what I want and how I want to be?
- What is holding me back from doing the things I love?
- Who do I find inspiring and what are the qualities I admire in them?
- Who do I have a reaction against and what are the qualities that repel me?

Germaine paused. She wanted to keep the relationship as it was, but she also wanted to feel more healthy and not be obliged to take stuff that didn't support that. 'I want to be myself,' she realised. And if she was really being herself she'd be able to tell Stefano what was going on. After all, what was the worst that could happen? She decided to talk to him the next day.

Somehow expressing her fear had already diminished its hold. Letting go of having to be a certain way had made her feel more free and less tense.

Going to the next question, she thought about what was really holding her back. Time was an excuse, so maybe it was apathy, or possibly she'd just got out of the habit. She struggled to reach an answer and moved on to the next question instead.

Who do I find inspiring? Steve Jobs. She wrote his name down and then an explanation: 'He had such vision, determination and rigour. He did things his way despite what anyone else thought of him.'

She was really getting through this now. 'OK, who do I have a reaction against and what are the qualities that repel me?' she thought, but she didn't like that question. She felt guilty that the person she immediately thought of was Mike. She tried to think of someone more remote, but she kept coming back to him.

'MIKE,' she wrote. 'Clinical. Smart in a cold detached way. Judgemental. Arrogant.'

'Was that right?' she wondered. Mike could be charming and kind, and who was she to judge?

~ 17 ~

Germaine was feeling stressed. She hated dealing with clients when they were making unreasonable demands or being overly picky. Owen had had an earful from the marketing manager at Gintech after some confusion over the brief, and she'd been asked to help smooth things over. She'd found herself on the defensive, but they had finally come to a satisfactory conclusion and a way forward without anyone losing face.

It was now 4:30 and she was tired and drained after the debrief with Owen and Dominic. Dominic had been his usual flamboyant self, quite prepared to give the client a piece of his mind for continually changing the brief without consultation. Owen had been pragmatic, despite being irritated with Gintech's attitude. Both had been complimentary about Germaine's handling of the situation.

She picked up the phone on the second ring. It was Ben. Out of the corner of her eye she could see Caroline, one of the junior account managers, approaching her desk. Seeing she was talking, Caroline made an apologetic gesture and thumbed towards the exit to indicate she was going. Germaine nodded, frowning. She half remembered a conversation about Caroline needing to leave early.

Ben was telling her that his dad had a cold and that for the first time he was really aware of his father looking old. Germaine was feeling old herself and said so.

When she put the phone down, she could see Mike heading over. There was something in his demeanour that made her heart sink.

'Germaine, can I have a word?' His voice was hard and cold.

'Sure, what's up?' Her first thought was, 'What have I done now?'

'I notice that's the second time in two weeks that Caroline's left early and there's nothing in the system,' said Mike.

Germaine could feel her cheeks flushing.

'It's not the first time,' he continued. 'The working hours are 8 till 6 for a reason. There are standards, and there are procedures to back up those standards.'

'She has a valid reason.' Germaine wished she could remember what that reason was, but she couldn't think clearly.

Mike ignored her. 'It's your responsibility to follow the procedures and make sure your team do as well. That's what a manager does.'

He paused for effect, then continued, 'If you disagree with the procedures you had a chance to say so at the meeting at the beginning of the year or at any time since. You know holidays and time off need to be requested by email, agreed by email and copied to Chloe and me. Procedures are part of the big-company mentality and it's the only way we will successfully manage our growth. Sending emails is not onerous – it's not like I'm asking you to fill out endless forms in triplicate.'

Germaine couldn't argue with the logic and she felt shut down and small. 'I'm sorry,' she heard herself say. She wanted to be able to disappear.

Mike broke the pregnant silence. 'That's OK. We just need to be on top of it, that's all. We don't want to send a message that it's acceptable for some people to bunk off early and not for others.'

The edge in his voice had gone and Germaine was relieved that he left it at that.

The conversation had obviously been louder in her mind than in reality, since when she looked around no one appeared to have noticed.

She searched her emails for anything Caroline had sent that might shed light on where she had gone. Then she remembered. Caroline was starting a six-week course and there was one evening session a week that she needed to attend. Germaine had given tacit agreement, but had forgotten to get her to make a formal request.

Thinking of how trivial this seemed fuelled her indignation. She got up from her desk and sought out Tom. 'I need a chat.'

Out of earshot of the office, Germaine let fly. 'Why is Mike such an arrogant shit?'

She explained what had happened, aware that she was embellishing it to make Mike seem even more of an arse and omitting his reasoning.

'That's awful,' said Tom. 'It looks like bullying to me. Maybe we should have a word with Jeremy.' He appeared concerned and outraged on her behalf.

Having vented her ire Germaine felt calmer, but the thought came to her that there was something for her to learn.

'I'm not being totally fair,' she admitted. 'I need to take some responsibility for this. Thanks for listening, though. Sorry for dumping on you.'

She felt stronger now that she'd spoken more truthfully and taken some responsibility for the events. Previously she would have happily spent half an hour bitching about Mike.

~ 18 ~

Later that night, back at her empty flat, Germaine still felt emotionally raw from her confrontation with Mike. She would have liked to talk it through with Ben and she felt his absence more keenly.

She kept replaying the scene in her mind and knew that the feelings it stirred up were out of proportion to the event itself. 'How funny that I was doubting the wisdom of putting Mike down as someone I was repelled by,' she thought.

She remembered Theo saying that there was no such thing as coincidence, there was meaning in everything. What was the meaning, though?

Her head buzzed. Thoughts like that could drive a person crazy.

She picked up her journal. She liked how it felt now: there was a familiarity in the process of opening it up and writing in it.

Theo had also said to look for herself in the person she was repelled by. What had she written about Mike? She checked: 'Clinical, smart in a cold detached way. Judgemental. Arrogant.'

'That's the opposite of me,' she thought. 'I would never treat someone like that, I wouldn't want to make anyone feel that uncomfortable.'

A ghost of a feeling threatened to break through and her stomach lurched as she thought of her dad. She could feel righteous indignation coming to greet her like an old friend. She got up suddenly, as if anxious to leave an unsafe space.

She went to the kitchen and made a beeline for the fridge. Opening a bottle of chilled white wine, she helped herself to a large glass and a hunk of extra mature Cheddar.

Returned to the sofa, she consciously ignored her journal and switched on the television. But channel surfing while nibbling her cheese and sipping her wine didn't help. She was agitated and found it hard to focus. She could feel a headache coming on.

'Look at you, you sad old tart,' she muttered out loud.

Germaine thought about calling Ben, but didn't want to sound feeble and needy.

She drained her glass and decided to treat herself to a long bath. Grabbing a headache pill from the bathroom cabinet, she turned on the taps and poured in some very expensive aromatic bath oil that Ben had bought her for Christmas. The scent reminded her of the spa she'd gone to in Thailand, and the bath started to assume a ceremonial aspect. She lit some large scented candles on the floor and tea lights around the rim of the bath like it was an altar to the god of bathing. Connecting her iPad to the speakers, she selected a playlist Ben had created for her last birthday. She hadn't got around to listening to it, but it seemed apt now.

When the bath was deep and the room suitably steamy, Germaine slipped into the water. She had turned the lights off and the candles created dancing shadows. She was struck by the timelessness of the scene.

The heat of the bath slowly drew out the aches and worries of the day. The slow, quiet music and flickering lights lulled her into a trancelike state. Then the lyrics of one song permeated her consciousness in waves: 'You go back to her, and I go back to black, black, black, black...'

The unmistakeable voice of Amy Winehouse made Germaine feel like crying again. The song was about betrayal – why had Ben put that on a playlist for her? Then she remembered that they had first really connected when they had talked about the tragedy of the singer's life. She had seen a different side to Ben beyond his laid-back persona.

She remembered him asking her about her parents and the first time she had confided in him about the pain she felt when her parents split up. Just thinking about it again brought a constriction in her chest and a lump to her throat. She had loved that Ben hadn't pressed her to reveal more or judged her, but now that just made her feel even more alone.

Theo's words 'What you resist shall persist' popped into her head unbidden, and she dropped under the surface of the bath, muffling out the music. Within moments the lack of air cleared her thoughts and she focused on the growing thump of her heart in her eardrums. She held on to her breath until the seconds stretched and so did her chest and head. Finally, the pain and urge for release grew too great and she broke the surface with a desperate gasp.

'What's wrong with me?' she thought. 'Get a grip.' But a chord had been struck deep within her and she felt its significance.

She tried to shut out thoughts of her dad and just listen to the music. Ben's selections were thoughtful and charted the ups and downs of their relationship. The memories the music evoked moved her and it eventually shifted her mood, as she appreciated the effort he had gone to for her. By the time the bath had cooled, Germaine felt drained but emotionally as well as physically cleaner, with a fresh resolve.

~ 19 ~

Germaine could see something was up by the way Mike was walking. His gaze was down and fixed ahead, his shoulders were tense and his stride was purposeful. The object of his focus was Jeremy, who was expansively gesturing while on the phone. Seeing Mike, he put his hand over the receiver, gestured two minutes and pointed to the nearest conference room.

Germaine was suddenly aware of the atmosphere. The other people in the office were whispering and watching the two men.

When Jeremy finished his call, he followed Mike into the conference room. The room was fairly well insulated, but raised voices could still be heard. Mike had obviously said something that had annoyed Jeremy, because the staff could see through the window that the MD's face was red and he was finger pointing. Mike then stood up and glared at Jeremy, who threw his hand up as if tossing an imaginary object towards the financial director.

Minutes later, they left the conference room and went to their respective desks. Germaine noticed that no one, not even Chloe, approached either of them for a while.

Later that afternoon she was distracted by the familiar ding of an instant message on her computer. From Jeremy, it read: 'Get Liam back to work.'

Germaine looked up and saw Liam chatting to one of the girls in planning. Turning towards Jeremy, she could see he was frowning. He made a thumbing motion as if to say 'shift it'.

Germaine could feel herself flush. She thought of replying on Instant Messenger, but decided against it.

She wasn't sure what she was feeling – a mixture of hurt, guilt and a tinge of anger.

'Liam, have you got a minute?' she called across to him. He smiled and walked over.

'What's up?'

Her mind raced, trying to think of the best way to handle the situation. She didn't want to put Liam on edge by telling him Jeremy was annoyed at him talking, but she did want to let him know he needed to be aware of the impact of what he was doing.

'I just wanted to check how it went with Simon at Livko.'

'Good. He tells me nothing's been finalised and I'll be one of the first to know when it is. In the meantime he's happy with our work and potentially has a couple of small side projects for us to do. In fact, I was just chatting with Sarah about some ideas.'

'Oh, it looked like you were flirting.'

Liam blushed. 'I don't follow what you mean.'

'Mike and Jeremy are on the warpath at the moment, so we need to look like we're getting our heads down. We don't want to give them anything to find fault with.'

'But I was working...' Liam protested.

'Let's leave it at that. I know you've done nothing wrong. Don't worry about it.'

Germaine was tense and could see that Liam was now upset. He returned to his desk, but his whole demeanour was down.

Feeling resentful against Jeremy, she decided to go out for some fresh air.

'Fancy a walk?' she asked Tom, who was walking past her desk.

'Sure. I've only got a few minutes though.'

'Argghh, that fucker!' hissed Germaine when they got in the lift.

'Who are you talking about?'

'Jeremy! He's such a controlling son of a bitch. Why doesn't he butt out. Everything was running smoothly and he has to get all moody and screw things up.'

'I know what you mean. I'm sure he doesn't realise he's doing it. He just gets a bee in his bonnet about something and pays no attention to the havoc he creates around him.'

They spent the next ten minutes walking round the block and listing all the things they hated about Jeremy and Mike's behaviour.

'Listen to us, we're a couple of old washerwomen,' Germaine laughed.

'Speak for yourself,' replied Tom in mock offence. 'Having a gripe isn't the province of women, men have been doing it for just as long.'

Germaine felt better after having got things off her chest, but the atmosphere was brittle when she returned to the office. For the first time in years she found herself clock watching. 'This is one for the journal,' she thought.

At six o'clock she started to pack up and noticed her team making moves in unison to leave as well. The one exception was Liam, who was immersed in something on his computer.

'Why don't you leave it till the morning?' Germaine asked.

He hardly looked up in acknowledgement. 'Not just yet. I've got a couple of things to sort out before tomorrow.'

Germaine didn't know what to do or say, so she left him to it.

When she was filling in her journal for that day, she wondered what to say about the episode with Jeremy and Liam. It was definitely an energy drain, but why? She wrote:

- ENERGY DRAIN – Jeremy butting in
- Being put on the spot
- Not being strong enough to say no
- Beating myself up for it

She thought about this for a while. The behaviour she could see was being submissive when confronted without being pre-armed. So what was the belief?

If it was that she needed to be pre-armed, that made no sense, as she should be able to think on her feet. She could picture Theo asking, 'What's behind that?'

Germaine struggled with this for a few minutes, then gave up. That was one for her next session tomorrow morning.

She turned the page in her journal. At the top was a picture of a lion cub on its back in a playful pose, as if anticipating an aerial attack.

~ 20 ~

'Anything we should talk about from the work you've been doing?' asked Theo when they met.

Germaine thought about the situation from the previous day with Jeremy and Liam, but didn't feel like dealing with it then. 'Not right now.' She half expected Theo to pick up on what she was thinking, but he seemed happy to continue without comment.

'Do you remember we talked about how important it is to have some idea of where you would like to go and what that looks like? A vision for yourself, if you will,' he began.

Germaine nodded – this was interesting.

'Good. What I'd like to do now is take you through a visualisation process. First, it's best to get into a very relaxed state.'

'Why do I need to be relaxed?'

'It gives you time to interact with your subconscious mind. In a relaxed or meditative state your subconscious gets to process events that happen during your waking hours and make connections that you perhaps wouldn't reach consciously.'

'OK, so what's visualisation all about?' Germaine asked.

'At the back of your journal there's a whole section of references about visualisation and meditation. Sportspeople employ visualisation to help them improve their performance, and neuroscientists have found that people who are considered charismatic leaders use visioning to create an exciting view of the future. It's not just about the visual, it's best if we involve all the senses and especially feeling.'

'What do I need to do?'

'Sit up straight but relaxed, with both your feet on the ground and your hands resting on your thighs. Close your eyes. I'll talk you through it. Now imagine a set of steps descending into a safe space, and walk down them.'

Theo's voice encouraged her to relax and reassured her that whatever she felt was just perfect. Germaine could picture the steps and after slowly descending to the bottom, she did feel wonderfully relaxed. She was on the edge of drifting off to sleep, but Theo kept her awake by giving her instructions.

'Go to a time in the future, near the end of your life,' he told her. 'You're looking back at your life and your challenges and successes. What might your older self want to say to you now with the wisdom of experience?' He paused to give her time, then went on, 'Now move to after your death, at your funeral. Who will be there and what will they be saying about you?'

At the end of the process, Theo brought her back up the steps and into the present moment.

'That was really dreamlike,' said Germaine. 'I knew what I was doing, but I wasn't worried about it.'

'Take a few minutes now to write down your challenges, successes, the wisdom of your future self, and the things people were saying about you,' Theo said.

Germaine had felt pride in having been a thought leader in the corporate world, speaking at large conferences. She had done it while balancing a rich home life. She had been an inspiration to women around the world. What had struck her most about her future self was how comfortable she had felt in her own skin. She could tell she loved her life and the people in it. Germaine felt she would really want to spend time with her future self, just hanging out. At her funeral there were people from work, family and friends. They were sad, but they were also celebrating her life and the impact she had had on them.

Thinking of the memory made Germaine bubble with an emotion akin to gratitude and joy. She noticed she had goosebumps.

When Germaine looked to have finished, Theo asked, 'So who were the significant people there?'

'Well, I got the sense that Ben was there and we had grown-up kids and they had kids too.' She felt warm at the thought, but also realised she held some fear about whether she would have a family.

'You frowned just then, disturbing what looked like a happy recollection,' Theo noted. 'What was that?'

'It's just I realised that I've been afraid I won't have a family and seeing them in the visualisation made me realise how important that is to me.'

'Shall we tap on that?'

Theo and Germaine did a few rounds of EFT to clear the fear. Afterwards Germaine wrote in her journal a commitment to tap on the fear of not having a family and whatever came up from that for the next few days.

'Who else was there?' Theo continued.

'People from work, clients and colleagues. All of them were great friends too.'

'You seem content that that's the case. What is it about the fact that your clients and colleagues are friends that's important?'

'I just felt that I could be truly myself and that they could be too. There was a freedom, a creativity that came with that.'

'So creativity, freedom, authenticity and relationship are all big values – that's great. Make a note of those, as they are key for you when making difficult decisions.'

Theo coached her around her vision, encouraging her to clarify and embellish it by mirroring back what she had said and asking her to elaborate.

'It sounds like you were a role model and able to use your experiences to help others have balance in their lives. Is balance another of your core values?'

'Yes, having been out of it for such a long time shows me that it is. I feel like I'm starting to move in the right direction, but I have a long way to go. It's like yesterday at work, there was an incident with Jeremy and Liam. Jeremy questioned my management because he thought Liam was wasting time, when in fact he was working, and Liam was resentful with me when I asked him about it. I tried to understand what was going on, but I got a bit stuck. I wasn't sure what the belief was behind the feeling.'

'So the feeling was submissive when confronted?'

'Yes.'

'Is it the same when you're confronted by anyone?'

Germaine paused, trying to think of any time she felt that way with women. 'No, thinking about it I guess not. I'd say it's men in authority.'

'You look like you've had a realisation,' said Theo, regarding her enquiringly.

'Yes, but I don't think I want to go there now.' She'd connected it with her father, but she didn't want to open that particular Pandora's box while at work.

'That's fine, Germaine. You do it at your own pace. Now, it seemed like there was a second element about your interaction with Liam.'

'Umm, yes. I think I was upset about being made to do something I didn't want to do and I knew it was wrong. It just made everything worse.'

'So it sounds like you didn't listen to your intuition and didn't do what you thought was right. It's not surprising it was upsetting, it was contrary to some of your core values. Did you feel like a victim?'

'I was forced into it. It wasn't how I would have handled it.' Germaine could hear the pleading in her voice and didn't like it, she thought she sounded weak.

'So you had no choice?' Theo asked.

'OK, I get it. Of course I had a choice. I just felt like I didn't.'

'It sounds like you had a subconscious belief playing out. Your values can be great allies in showing up what you need to look at – especially beliefs. What might the belief be in this case?'

'It's the same old stuff I think, that I'm not good enough.'

'Shall we tap and see where that goes?'

They did a few more rounds of EFT and this time Theo added a couple of rounds of affirmations at the end: 'I own my power as a woman' and 'I love myself unconditionally'.

At the end of the session Germaine felt grounded and full of purpose. 'Now let Jeremy try to call me out,' she thought.

~ 21 ~

The following week at work, Germaine noticed she was feeling more self-assured and she seemed to be attracting fewer angry men. She couldn't put it down purely to the coaching, but she thought maybe there was a link. Perhaps how she felt inside really did have an impact on what happened around her.

She was musing over the implications one morning when she turned the corner into the office and there stood Liam. He seemed upset and wouldn't look directly at her.

'You OK?' she asked.

He shook his head.

'Do you want to go somewhere for a chat?' Germaine offered.

Liam just nodded.

'Let's get out of the office. That OK with you?'

They left work and crossed the street to Dixies. Stefano greeted them and took their order.

Once they were sat in a quiet corner, Germaine waited for Liam to speak. After what felt like minutes but was probably tens of seconds, she could bear it no longer. 'So, Liam, you look upset – what's going on?'

Liam swallowed and glanced up. Germaine could see the hurt in his eyes and dreaded what he was about to say.

'My dad died at the weekend,' he told her.

Germaine's first fleeting emotion was relief that it hadn't been about what had happened the previous week at work. That feeling was hastily replaced with empathy for what Liam must be going through, and a little guilt.

'Oh my God, I can't believe that, Liam. Why didn't you say anything? I'm so sorry. Were you close?'

'Very. My mum died five years ago and he took it badly, but he seemed to be finding his feet again. It was such a shock.'

'That's got to be tough. My dad died when I was 21, but we weren't close...' She stopped – why was she talking about herself?

Liam looked like a lost soul and was absently tearing the corners of a postcard that had been left on the table.

'You must take some time off. I can hardly believe you're here,' Germaine told him.

'I've got a lot of stuff to do and I thought it might help to think about something else, but I'm finding it hard to focus. It's all a bit surreal, like I'm not really here and it's happening to someone else. You know what I mean?'

'I think so,' Germaine said, but she wasn't sure she did. She often felt a little spaced out due to exhaustion and overstimulation, but she suspected he was talking about something else.

'Do you need any help?' she went on. 'Are your notes up to date so Katherine and I can handle your work?'

'Yes, pretty much. I've been involving Ellie the newbie recently, so she'll be able to help too. The funeral's on Wednesday, so I should be back Thursday or Friday if that's OK.'

'I really think you should take the whole week off, Liam. Whatever you need, please just let us know.'

Her heart went out to him and she felt like giving him a hug, but wasn't sure if it was appropriate.

~ 22 ~

Liam's absence forced Germaine to help more in day-to-day operations. Luckily, she'd started to push back on meetings a bit and delegate more to Owen and Katherine, to help them to develop, and now she realised the benefits of being able to look at the team from a more detached position.

She was determined to get out and enjoy her week-ends. Keeping her journal had shown her how much she had been missing out on due to being overly focused on work. One Saturday she persuaded Ben to take a trip to Borough Market. She had a slight headache that she assumed was due to too much red wine the night before, but they set off bright and early without hassle.

They got on the tube at Turnham Green and found it surprisingly busy for a weekend morning. Germaine jumped in and grabbed two seats together by the doors, sitting down with visible relief after checking the seat for any dodgy stains. Ben followed in a more relaxed fashion.

Germaine looked up to check out the people around her and suddenly felt dizzy. Her temples were thudding. She closed her eyes, massaging her temples with the heels of her thumbs.

'Are you alright?'

She could hear the concern in Ben's voice and feel the warmth of his hand on her shoulder. She tried to breathe deeply and open her eyes.

'My head's splitting. I think it's getting worse.' The world seemed a blur. Her heart started to pound in time with her temples, her vision misted and the noises around her seemed far away. She had a memory of being put under by gas at the dentist's and the sound of an echoey swimming pool, and then there was nothing...

'Germaine! Germaine! Hey, Germaine, it's Ben. Are you with us?'

She opened her eyes and saw Ben and a bunch of strangers peering at her with concerned and curious expressions.

'Do you need some water?' asked a smartly dressed young man.

'What happened?' she asked.

'You passed out for a minute or so. How's your headache?'

'Not as bad, but it still hurts.'

'I think we need to skip the market and find an A&E.'

'I'll be fine – I just need a minute.'

'Let's get off at Hammersmith, go for a walk and see how you are.'

'OK.' Germaine didn't much feel like going to the market now anyway. She watched a moth flutter by, hit against the window and continue to fly up and down behind her.

'It's the next station.' Ben leaned over to pick up her bag. 'I'll carry this.'

When the train stopped, Germaine hauled herself to her feet, making sure she held on to Ben's arm just in case she was still dizzy. The last thing she wanted was to fall over and embarrass herself. She felt better when she got off the train into the air.

They found a café just up King Street. After collecting her thoughts for a while and sipping her fruit smoothie, the shock of what had happened crept up on Germaine. She was worried there was something seriously wrong with her.

Ben persuaded her she should see a doctor. 'Charing Cross Hospital is just down the road, we could walk there. At least they'd give us an idea of what's up, without having to wait till Monday to see your GP.'

'I can't go on Monday anyway, I've got a very important client meeting. OK, let's go to the hospital now.'

When at last her name was called, a tall nurse with chestnut hair, a husky voice and a gentle smile started to quiz her, first making sure Germaine had had no impacts to her head or spine recently. Then she asked her about the episode itself. 'Has this ever happened before? Any dizzy spells, headaches?'

The nurse took her blood pressure. 'It's a little on the low side, so the most likely diagnosis is orthostatic hypotension. That's something you should definitely check out with your GP, but I'm pretty confident that it's not life threatening at the moment so I'm happy for you to be discharged.'

~ 23 ~

The following week at work Germaine was busy with pitches and she managed to put her blackout to the back of her mind. Then on Thursday morning she had a nightmare. A shadowy figure had been chasing her through darkened streets. She had the nagging feeling she knew the person and wanted to be able to turn and look at him, but was too afraid to stop. She woke in a state of panic, her head and heart pounding.

She made enough of a commotion to stir even Ben from his sleep. He rolled over and asked with eyes still shut, 'You OK? Wassup?'

'Just a bad dream,' Germaine replied, turning on the light. A vestige of fear lingered in her mind. She listened a while for any noises in the flat, then looked at the alarm clock. It said 6:05 am. 'Near enough time anyway,' she thought as she slipped out of bed.

In the bathroom she poured a glass of water, reached for the mirrored cabinet door, and peered at her reflection. She had expected to look worse. Her eyes were a tad darker than she would have liked, but considering the percussion going on in her head and the quality of last night's sleep, she was pleasantly surprised.

She opened the cabinet and grabbed the Nurofen packet. She popped two pills into her mouth and as she chased it down with water, the words 'Give us our daily bread' popped into her mind. She would have laughed if her head hadn't hurt so much.

That ritual complete, she showered, dressed, applied her make-up and went into the kitchen. A cup of tea and a bowl of fruit, yoghurt and muesli were now part of her regime. It reminded her of breakfasts on her all-time favourite holiday in Thailand.

She found eating harder going this morning, though. Her headache was sapping the memory, the taste and the pleasure from the experience. After a couple of spoonfuls, she put the bowl aside and drank her tea.

She took out her journal and entered what she'd eaten and how she felt. She looked at the butterfly picture at the front again, breathed deeply and sat listening to the sounds of the house and the muffled noises from the street outside. By the time Ben had got up and she needed to leave for work, her headache had again receded to a bearable dullness with an occasional sharp pang. She knew she should go to her GP, but she didn't have the time.

Around lunchtime she was finding it hard to concentrate at work and felt a little nauseous, so she went to the toilet to freshen up. She splashed water on her face and looked in the mirror. Her reflection was a little blurred and as she leaned forward to get a better look, she noticed her field of vision was getting tighter and tighter and darkness was closing in. She felt her legs going and then nothing.

She was aware of water trickling and the lights on the ceiling, one of which needed replacing. The cold pressure of the floor tiles against her head and back informed her she was lying down. What the hell was happening to her?

She sat up and felt the back of her head. There was no blood or discernible lump, so she must have avoided cracking her head in her fall. Despite feeling shocked and embarrassed, she was otherwise feeling OK. Her headache had receded again to a dull ache.

Clambering to her feet, she splashed her face, fixed her make-up, took a deep breath and went back to the office.

No one appeared to have noticed her absence. She sat at her desk and thought about pretending that nothing had happened, then she realised that was ridiculous. She went to find a quiet spot where she could phone Ben without being overheard.

'Hi Ben,' she said when he answered. 'Don't be alarmed, but I passed out again.'

He let her know in no uncertain terms that she had to phone her GP and ask for a referral for further tests. Dr Eccles agreed to see her that afternoon.

She went to Jeremy to let him know she needed the afternoon off. She dreaded telling him, particularly because her team was understaffed at the moment. She thought somehow that she was letting people down and she felt guilty. She knew it was illogical, but she couldn't shake it, so she tapped the points as Theo had instructed until she felt calmer.

To her surprise, Jeremy was completely supportive and concerned about her. She didn't tell him about the blackouts, only that she'd been having headaches and the doctor wanted to see her. Jeremy's opinion was that it was probably overwork and that she should take it easy for a while, maybe coming in later a couple of days a week. She was taken aback and joked that Mike wouldn't appreciate the flagrant breach of the company handbook.

'Let me take care of Mike,' said Jeremy warmly. 'He's not as devoid of empathy as he'd like you to think.'

~ 24 ~

As Germaine walked into Chiswick Health Centre, she felt a strange sense of dread. Dr Eccles was nice enough, but on many occasions she'd considered changing to a female doctor, although she chided herself for being sexist.

'So what can I do for you?' her GP asked, glancing at his computer screen and then back to Germaine.

'Well, it's probably nothing, but I've been having headaches for a while and recently I've had a couple of blackouts.'

The doctor raised his eyebrows and Germaine thought he looked a lot like an actor playing a person in authority. 'Can you describe these blackouts? What were you doing and what were the sensations?'

He took notes on what she said. 'What about the headaches, is there any pattern to their occurrence? Does anything you do make them better or worse?'

'I'm not aware of any particular pattern, and actually I've had fewer recently. Lying down or painkillers are the only things that help at all,' Germaine told him.

'Can you tell me about your general health? Are you eating and sleeping well?'

'I'm sleeping a lot better than I have for a long time and I'm eating more healthily. That's what I'm confused by.'

'I see on your records that last year you were prescribed some sleeping pills. Have you had the problem since then?'

'For a few months.' Germaine understated the problem and felt guilty that her GP wasn't aware that she'd had difficulty sleeping for a number of years. 'It's been better for a month or so now.'

'And have you been particularly stressed at work?'

'It is stressful, but I don't know many well-paid jobs that aren't. I think I've turned a corner in that respect and I'm handling the stress better.'

'I see.' His eyebrows elevated again. 'If you don't mind I'd like to do a few tests.'

He proffered a hand and added, 'Can you squeeze my hand with your left hand?'

Germaine took his hand, conscious of the heat of it. She squeezed as directed.

'Good... and now with your right, please.'

After she'd complied, the doctor took a rubber hammer from a desk drawer and went on, 'Can you cross your legs?' He tapped her knee and then repeated the procedure for the other leg.

After making a few notes on the computer, he produced a tiny little light and shone it in her eyes.

Germaine was aware that she was breathing in his breath and had the urge to pull away.

'Can you follow this light without moving your head?' he asked as he stood up and moved the light from left to right and back again.

When he put her through even more tests, Germaine wondered if he was making some of them up to see how far she would go.

'Close your eyes and repeat after me: "Cheese, chair, nose, light, door".'

Feeling like he was taking the piss, she did so.

'Good. Now would you mind removing your top?'

She meekly complied, but couldn't look him in the eye as he gently prodded her abdomen and looked under her armpits.

'Can you remove your bra too?'

Germaine could sense herself flush, but did so, feeling very self-conscious. Dr Eccles proceeded to prod and squeeze her breasts.

'Do you examine your breasts regularly?' he asked.

'Not really.' Her voice was constrained and her mouth dry.

'There are lumps, which is normal, but it would be a good idea for you to get familiar with your breasts so that you notice if anything changes. Are these areas very sensitive?'

'Not really, no.' Germaine wanted the experience to end as quickly as possible.

'You can put your things back on,' said the doctor eventually. 'I don't think there's anything to worry about, but I'm going to refer you to a specialist. It may take a while unless you go privately. Do you have health cover?'

'Yes, through work.' She wondered why she felt guilty.

~ 25 ~

The specialist's office was near Harley Street. While the building was grand, the interior was tired and uninspiring. Germaine thought it seemed more like a student bedsit than an office, but then stopped herself – who cared what it looked like?

She was feeling anxious, a bit like she was interviewing for a job she wasn't qualified for. Sitting in reception with Ben, her mind strayed to work. She'd been scheduled to have a meeting with Liam and a couple of the team at Livko, but had asked Dominic to go in her place. He had texted her last night that Owen was going instead, and she was worried she had been outmanoeuvred for some reason.

'I really do need my head examining,' she thought. 'Here I am at a brain specialist and I'm worrying about my job.'

A young man came in and talked to the receptionist in a hushed voice. She indicated for him to sit down. He was perhaps in his early twenties and looked a bit dishevelled and hungover, his face ashen. He varied from sitting with his eyes closed to bending over with his head in his hands. Germaine wondered what his story was.

Dr Reas's office was a little more stylish, although possibly too minimalist for Germaine's liking.

'Did your GP give you a physical exam?' asked the specialist after they'd discussed why the referral had been made.

'Yes, he did. He gave me a breast exam and I wasn't sure whether that was necessary...' Germaine told her.

'Did he give you a rectal exam too?'

'No, should he have?' said Germaine, thinking she was grateful he hadn't.

'Well, if there was any suspicion of cancer that would have been thorough. You see, cancer in the brain is more likely to be a secondary tumour, so one that has originated elsewhere such as in the breast or digestive system. Did your GP not explain any of this?'

Germaine felt a little ashamed for doubting Dr Eccles, although she also realised she was resentful and a bit angry when she recalled the occasion.

After her own examination Dr Reas said, 'I think we need to get you along for a scan. I will see if I can get you one today or tomorrow. Is that OK with you?'

'What do you think it is?' Germaine and Ben asked simultaneously.

'That's what we're going to try to find out – a scan will give us a better idea.'

Germaine felt a touch of dread.

She was in and out of the scan without waiting and hardly spoke to anyone throughout. She just filled out a form, was given a brief description about what to do for the scan itself and then was 'processed' without fuss. She was back at work in just over an hour and acted as if nothing had happened.

~ 26 ~

The following evening, Germaine and Ben were sitting in the living room. He'd been off work with a bit of a cold, so she'd been his nurse, a role she felt pleased with herself for playing.

'You can watch the footie if you want,' Germaine graciously offered.

'It's OK, its only Spurs tonight, my team aren't playing. What do you want to watch?' Ben proffered the remote.

'I don't know, what's on?'

'We could watch a film, maybe look at what's new?' Ben said between bouts of blowing his nose.

'OK, but you do it, I never know how to use this thing.' She gave the remote back.

Ben smiled, raising his eyebrows in mock despair. 'If you don't try you'll never learn.'

He was flicking through the latest releases when the phone rang.

Germaine debated whether to leave it. Most people rang her mobile, so it was probably a sales call.

'Can you get that ?' Ben asked, still focused on the list on the screen.

Germaine checked the caller ID, which said 'Withheld'. She picked the receiver up on a whim, expecting the person on the other end to hang up almost immediately.

'Hello?' It was a woman's voice, one she didn't quite recognise.

'Hi, this is Germaine, who's that?'

'Hi, Germaine, sorry to call you in the evening. It's Dr Reas.'

Germaine's heart dropped into her stomach.

Ben looked up and asked with concern in his voice, 'What's up?'

'What's wrong? Did the scan show something?' Germaine could hear the tremor in her own voice.

'I don't want to discuss it over the phone, but I would like to see you as soon as possible. Can you come in tomorrow morning at 10 or 10:30?'

Germaine felt light-headed and really scared. 'What is it? What's wrong with me? Is it serious?'

Ben had come over and put his hand on her shoulder. 'What's up? Who is it?'

'I don't want you to worry or get upset,' said Dr Reas. 'We'll discuss it tomorrow. I am sorry, I can't say any more right now. Is 10 o'clock at my office OK?'

'Yes, OK, bye.' Germaine replaced the phone. Her mind was blank, her body heavy and her head felt light. She fought the urge to be sick.

'What's going on, is what serious? Are you alright?' Ben asked, a bit frantic.

'It was Dr Reas, she's got the scans,' said Germaine, her voice hollow. 'She wants to see me tomorrow. It must be serious otherwise she wouldn't have called in the evening... I've got cancer.'

'Did she say that? Oh God...'

'No, she didn't, but what else could it be?'

'I don't know, but there's no point thinking the worst.' Ben's pale face belied his words.

With that Germaine began to cry and Ben did too. After a while they stopped and just held each other, feeling their breathing and heartbeat.

Germaine felt trapped, unable to think clearly. There was nothing she could do and she had no energy to do it anyway.

'Can I get you anything? Tea, water... something stronger?' Ben asked, his cold forgotten and the roles reversed.

'No, I think I might go to bed.' She was suddenly dog tired.

'You feeling OK?' She could see that Ben regretted the question as soon as he had said it.

They both slept fitfully, and in the taxi to the specialist's office in the morning Germaine felt detached, as if her body was on automatic and she was a casual observer.

'I'm sorry to call you in at such short notice. I know it must have been a bit of a shock,' Dr Reas began.

Germaine's heart missed a beat at the word 'shock'.

'Is it serious?' Ben asked, unable to hold himself back.

'Well, we don't entirely know. We did find a reasonably large dark patch on the left hemisphere...'

Germaine could feel the blood drain from her face. 'Is it cancer?' She voiced her greatest fear.

'I can't say for sure, but in my experience it's best to be prepared for the worst. It looks like there is a tumour, although that doesn't necessarily mean cancer. To be certain I'd like to do some further tests, as soon as possible.'

Germaine couldn't stop the tears and started sobbing.

'What are the tests?' Ben asked.

'Further scans and possibly a biopsy.'

'So what would the scans tell us and what are the risks?' The promise of action seemed to give him strength.

'Obviously there are low levels of radiation involved in the scans so we don't want to do too many, but the risks are small in comparison with what we are dealing with. They will give us a greater understanding of what's going on, as well as the precise location of activity. This will determine whether surgery is possible or whether other treatments are more suitable.'

'And the biopsy?' Ben probed, his brow furrowed in an unconscious response.

'That's a difficult question and the answer very much depends on what we're dealing with. If it's benign and not growing, it might be better to wait and see... but given that you've been getting headaches, Germaine, and have started to get blackouts, it would suggest there's some movement. We might have to take immediate action.'

The look in her eyes told Germaine that Dr Reas wasn't telling them the whole story.

~ 27 ~

Back in the cold October air, Germaine was hit by the unreality of her situation. The sky was bright blue. People were scurrying about their business. Life was continuing as normal, except everything had changed.

'You're going to get through this, I promise you,' said Ben, attempting to comfort her.

She realised he was trying to be strong for her, but she knew him well enough to see through the act. He was as frightened as she was.

'I don't want to die, I'm too young,' she sobbed. 'It's so unfair. Why is this happening? I can't believe it...'

Ben pulled her to him and hugged her. She was rigid at first, but yielded slowly to his warmth.

'Hey, Ben,' said a boy who had been walking past.

Ben turned his head and peered down at the boy. 'Oh, Prem. Sorry, I was miles away. It's a bit of a difficult time, we just had some bad news...'

Prem, Germaine realised, was not in fact a boy but a diminutive, fresh-faced man of indiscernible age and Southeast Asian origin.

'Oh, I'm sorry to hear that. I saw you were busy, but I couldn't not stop and say hi. You see, I was thinking of you just yesterday and then here you are.' Prem smiled.

'I should introduce you – this is Germaine,' said Ben. 'Prem and I worked on a project a few years back. He's a Buddhist and we did a few meditation classes together too.'

Surprising herself, Germaine said, 'Hello. What Ben means about a bad time is that we've just learned I've got a brain tumour.' There was something about Prem that made it OK to tell him.

'Sounds testing,' he acknowledged. His soft eyes spoke more than his words. 'Though things may not be as they seem...' He paused and then his face lit up. 'You know, there's a friend of mine who deals with this sort of thing, from an emotional perspective. She's appeared in several magazines and even on TV. You might have heard of her, Susan Watts. She does something called "The Journey". She swears by it.'

He smiled again as if waiting for recognition, but none was forthcoming. Unphased, he continued, 'I hope you don't mind me saying, but I've got a sense that she could be very helpful to you.' He offered Germaine his card and then turned back to Ben. 'We should meet up some time for a proper catch-up.'

Prem gave Germaine a quick hug and continued on his way.

Something had shifted for Germaine, although she wasn't quite sure what yet. 'You know, I don't think I will go to work today,' she said.

Ben laughed. 'You must be mad, of course you're not going.'

'I need some air,' Germaine continued. 'Do you mind if we go to Richmond Park for a walk? It's cold but it's so beautiful at this time of year.'

On the way to the tube she noticed a bookshop. 'Ben, do you mind if we just pop in there a minute?'

'Of course not. You go ahead, I'm going to phone work and tell them I'm not going to make it back today. Do you want me to call your office too?'

'Thanks.' She was so glad he was there with her. She needed him more than ever.

As she walked through the door, her eye was drawn by a large black-and-white photo of a middle-aged woman standing in the sea with her arms aloft, looking as if she had just completed a Channel crossing. The look on her face was a mixture of elation, pride and, to Germaine's mind, disbelief.

A sign proclaimed a third off or two for the price of one. Germaine inspected the pile of books and lifted the first one, *I Will Not Die an Unlived Life* by Dawna Markova.

'I think I must be going mad, everything is talking to me,' she thought.

She started the first chapter to get a sense of the writing style. She read: 'I wrote this poem the night my father died with a shrug. His heart was hollow and vacant of dreams. He was convinced he didn't matter.'

Germaine felt a twinge of distaste for the man, but also intrigued, so she read on: 'I got out of bed, carting my journal over to the old mahogany desk that had been my father's. I could feel the river swelling in my heart. As I sat down, it flowed out of my hand. The tears had turned to ink. The words were a bridge across an abyss my father could not cross. They were his blessing to me.'

She could feel a strange mix of emotions – repulsion, yet attraction. Flicking to the back cover, she saw there was a poem. She read some of the lines: 'I will not live in fear of falling or catching fire', 'I choose to risk my significance'.

She felt like someone had run a cold finger down her back. The poem seemed like a message sent directly to her.

Germaine was about to go and pay for the book when she noticed another one next to it called *The Journey*. She remembered Prem having mentioned the title, and decided she may as well buy that one as well.

~ 28 ~

Germaine was sitting on the sofa while Ben was preparing a late lunch. Left alone with her thoughts, her mind wouldn't settle.

'I've got cancer,' she thought, and her heart started to race. 'What if they operate and it leaves me a vegetable, or severely handicapped? I can't believe this is happening to me.'

She felt trapped with nowhere to run. The calm place of trust she had found at the park had been disturbed like a pebble hitting a still pool.

She got up and went over to the window. Her journal was on the sill. She picked it up, but then put it down again. What use was doing that stuff now she was ill?

She remembered Theo talking about stress: 'It's not what happens to you, it's how you deal with it.' That was easy for him to say.

He had talked many times about writing in her journal to help clear her mind of unwanted thoughts and emotions. She'd been doing that quite often at night and had found it helpful in getting off to sleep.

She fetched a pen from the table and picked up the journal again.

'OK, here goes,' she thought, and started writing: 'I'm going to die a horrible death... I'm going to be brain damaged... I'll never marry... I'll never give Ben kids... I'll never have kids... I'll never have kids...'

She began to cry, but continued to write. She knew it was illegible but she didn't care. Six pages later, she dropped the pen to the floor, lifted her feet onto the sofa and wound herself into a ball, crying softly.

Ben came in with her lunch to find her still curled up like a foetus, fast asleep, with make-up smeared over her face. He covered her with a blanket and left her to sleep.

When she woke up, he was looking at the books she'd bought.

'*The Journey*, wasn't that the thing Prem mentioned?' Ben asked.

'That's spooky,' she said. 'You know I think Theo originally recommended the book. Can you pass me my bag? I think I've still got the card he gave me.'

Sure enough, 'Susan Watts, Journey therapist' was written on the card. Germaine had the feeling of something clunking into place. 'Wasn't Susan Watts the name Prem mentioned too? She's in Eversley. How far is that?' she asked.

'No idea, why?'

'I think I need to go and see her.'

~ 29 ~

Germaine was nervous. She knew her driving was erratic, but the narrow country roads to the Hampshire village of Eversley were thankfully clear. Her SatNav politely informed her she was at her destination in a stilted American accent.

Susan Watts' house was a three-bed detached with a 'secret garden' feel to it. A loamy smell greeted Germaine as she walked up the gravel path, and she could see hanging baskets filled with winter flowers and plants.

She rang the bell, which prompted an enthusiastic bout of barking. A few seconds later a melodious voice called from within, 'Billy… Come… Here boy… Good boy… I'm here now.'

The door opened and a woman in her early fifties greeted Germaine.

'Don't mind Billy, he won't bother you. He's just curious,' Susan explained as the red setter planted his nose in Germaine's crotch. 'Are you OK with dogs?'

'I love them,' replied Germaine, giving Billy a scratch behind his ear.

'So do I – I'd have more but my husband doesn't think it's practical and I guess I have to agree with him.' Susan laughed ruefully. 'Come on through.'

They went to a homely room at the back of the house and Susan pointed to a comfortable-looking armchair. 'Sit down, please. Would you like tea or water? Or both?'

Germaine sank into the chair. 'A peppermint tea would be great, thanks.'

The window framed an old oak tree in the garden. A squirrel was chasing up and down, twitching its tail.

Susan could be heard shooing Billy and clanking around in the kitchen. It was such a comforting domestic sound, and the quality of the air made it sound even better. Germaine was at ease, more at home than she'd felt for a long time.

When Susan returned with the tray of drinks, she placed it on a coffee table and moved her own chair close to Germaine's.

'Now, I know you gave me a bit of background on the phone, but I'd like to get a clearer picture of what's going on for you and then I will explain the process a bit,' she began.

Gently and unemotionally, Susan pulled out the details, allowing Germaine to unravel the tangle of her fears, arriving finally at the reason she had chosen to visit.

'So, do you mind me asking about your father and mother?' Susan asked.

Germaine could feel the tension build in her throat and heart, and her breathing quicken. 'My dad died a few years ago. We weren't close though,' she said slowly.

'Sorry to hear that. And your mother?'

'She's OK, but I'm not sure she's ever recovered from the divorce. They split when I was twelve. She says she's fine, but I think she's lonely.'

'Is the break-up the reason you and your father weren't close?'

Germaine's chest tightened and she felt a little dizzy. She took a drink and marshalled her thoughts.

'Partly, but looking back I'm sure he was distancing himself before that.' An image of her father and the cold disappointment on his face came to her as clear as day. The shame she had felt as an eleven-year-old flooded back. Tears formed at the corners of her eyes.

'Is there a specific memory you're experiencing, Germaine?'

'I was caught stealing some make-up,' she explained. 'I felt bad about it, but it was my father's reaction I remember. He didn't get angry but just held my gaze, shook his head and turned away. It was an unspoken rebuke that hit harder than a slap and I cried myself to sleep that night.'

Susan used the same staircase technique as Theo had done to take Germaine to a place where she felt resourceful, encouraging her to build a picture of her safe space by involving all her senses. 'Is there water?' she asked. 'What does it sound like? Are you sitting or standing? What is the ground like beneath you? Can you feel any textures? What can you smell?'

Germaine pictured herself sitting on a little island, a flowering cherry tree at her back. Its branches gently moved in the lightest of breezes, which caused the sun to dance and dapple on her skin. The sun warmed her heart and she felt held.

'You are in total control here, Germaine, nothing can come here without your say-so. Now, I'd like you to introduce your painful memory, but in an abstract form, like a shape.'

Germaine put her memory in a black balloon floating on the other side of the stream that separated the stairs and her island. Slowly, Susan encouraged her to bring the balloon closer, checking whether it had changed at all. When it was near enough for Germaine to touch and feel no threat from it, Susan asked, 'Are you OK to look inside the balloon?'

Germaine felt uncomfortable, but was also intrigued, so she nodded.

'Look inside the balloon and see the scene with your dad playing out in miniature, like on a small TV. You are there as a little girl.'

Germaine replayed the scene as she remembered it, seeing her father's reaction and how the girl shut down.

'Now you are the director of this episode. Give the girl anything you feel might help her, or perhaps there's something you want to say to her.'

Germaine's heart went out to that little girl. 'It's OK. I love you. It might be a bad thing you did, but you're not bad. You're beautiful and I love you.'

She imagined the girl hearing those words and growing in stature, meeting her father's stare and seeing a hint of admiration in his eyes at her spirit as he turned away.

Had that been there all along? Had she been blind to it?

Germaine felt as if a great weight had been lifted from her chest and throat. She let out a sigh.

'Where's the balloon?' Susan asked.

'It's over on the other side of the stream again, but it's no longer a balloon, it's a shadowy figure. I can't see the face but I know it's my dad.' Germaine felt safe, but had no desire to let him any closer.

'Is there something you would like to say to your dad?' Susan asked.

'No,' said Germaine firmly, her voice like a shut door.

Susan didn't dwell on the father but reinforced the feelings of love and acceptance for the eleven-year-old Germaine. She guided her out of her safe space and back into the present and the room they were sat in. The time had flown and Germaine could hardly believe how long the process had taken.

'Would you like some lunch?' Susan asked after leaving her to gather her thoughts for a few minutes.

'Yes, that would be wonderful, thanks.' Germaine felt lighter and more energised.

'It's salad, nothing fancy I'm afraid,' said Susan when she returned from the kitchen with a large wooden bowl and two blue-and-white plates. 'Oh, I forgot the bread,' she added. 'Give me two secs.'

She disappeared into the kitchen again while Germaine helped herself to salad. Susan returned with some home-made bread, broke off a fist-sized chunk and passed it to Germaine. Something about the gesture, so effortless and timeless, struck Germaine and made her feel very grateful.

'So what's your connection with Theo? Did he coach you?' she asked Susan.

'In a way, but maybe not in the way you're thinking. Let's just say that Theo came into my life when I was at a crossroads and somehow he helped me choose my way. By doing so I think he learned something about himself.'

Germaine was curious, but didn't think she could push for any more.

After lunch, Susan asked if she would like a closer look at the garden. 'Some people wait till spring and summer to enjoy the outdoors, but they miss out on so much. We're so lucky here, such diversity. Most things can find some spot to grow.'

They spent the next half hour chatting about dogs, life, holidays and their passions while wandering around the garden. Susan bent down intermittently to weed or point out a particular plant, telling Germaine its story or an interesting fact about it. 'Sometimes when things aren't obvious there's real magic and joy in their discovery,' she said cryptically.

'I wish I knew more about this stuff. I didn't realise how interesting it was,' said Germaine, smiling apologetically.

'We all have our passions and interests. I've no doubt if I visited you at work and saw you in action I'd probably want to be able to do what you were doing,' Susan said. 'You might not guess it, but in an earlier life I was in high finance and I was very attracted to the buzz of the corporate world.'

Germaine thought she caught a wistful look in Susan's eyes and she was curious. 'Was that the crossroads you talked about?'

'Aren't you the clever one? You're naturally intuitive, aren't you? Yes, it was a difficult time for me. I had to make some hard choices and through that process I found my life.'

Stamping down some earth from an uprooted weed, she smiled and turned, beckoning Germaine back to the house.

When they resumed their session, Susan guided Germaine back to her safe place at the bottom of the staircase and asked her to think of a significant memory of her father. Germaine immediately became aware of the shadowy figure and experienced a visceral feeling of guilt and shame.

'Put the feelings in balloons and move them to a distance that you're comfortable with,' Susan said. 'What's the memory?'

'It was when my parents told me they were getting a divorce.'

'OK, replay the memory as if it's a video and you're the director again, observing the scene unfold.'

Germaine watched her father and mother sitting opposite her and explaining how they weren't getting on any more and her dad was going to live somewhere else. She could see the tension between her parents and remembered that she felt wrong somehow. Her father wasn't looking at her or her mother. Her mother was looking at her, trying to be strong, but her tears were betraying her. 'It's not your fault. Your dad will still see you. We both still love you,' her mother was saying.

Germaine remembered her dad's sad face and the way her heart pounded and her stomach churned. She realised she'd taken that look of sadness and wrapped her guilt and shame in it to make it a look of disapproval and disappointment. That realisation shocked her. It felt like something had come apart within her.

'Replay the scene, but this time change the perspective to your mother's and then one more time to your father's,' Susan suggested.

At each replay of the video Germaine felt less emotional attachment to the scene and Susan encouraged her to add new details. She acknowledged there were an array of emotions involved and she had a choice about which ones to access.

A memory of Theo saying 'It's not what happens to you, it's how you see it' flashed up in her mind.

Finally, Susan asked Germaine to remember the scene as she was as a twelve-year-old. This time the shame and fear were accompanied by a host of other emotions and she felt safe, as if her hand was being held. She could feel the shadowy figure pressing on her and the fear associated with it growing, but at the same time it was counterbalanced by the assurance received from her hand.

Germaine wondered if Susan was actually holding her hand at that moment as it felt so real, but she didn't open her eyes to check.

The shadowy figure took his rightful place at the table as she was replaying the scene and Germaine's eyes lowered, picking out the details of her hands clasped together, fingers chasing the blood from her flesh.

'This is it.' The words her mum said echoed in her ears. She could feel her tears building, her neck muscles taut, resisting the inevitable look at the face of the shadowy figure. When she glanced up, a hand wiped the tears from her eyes to reveal the sad face of her father. His lips were mouthing 'So sorry'.

A sob broke from somewhere deep inside her. It felt like a howling wind ripping at her insides. The tears poured out and she gasped, desperate for air, realising she'd been holding her breath. 'Did I cry back then?' she wondered.

When the storm had calmed and the tears subsided, Susan invited Germaine to say something to her twelve-year-old self.

'I forgive you. I love you. You are wonderful.'

'Would you like to say something to your mother then?'

'I forgive you. I know you did your best... and I love you.'

'And your father?'

Germaine breathed deeply. 'I'm sorry...' The tears came again. 'I'm sorry that I sometimes disappointed you and that I wasn't perfect but I was a child... I was learning... I am angry that you left.' With the words came a swelling of anger. 'I hated you... You left me... I was fucking twelve and you left me feeling it was me...'

Her father's face mouthing 'So sorry' replayed in her mind's eye over and over until Germaine realised she was whispering it herself. The anger had gone as quickly as it had come.

'I forgive you and I love you,' she said aloud. She felt as if a great weight had been lifted from her. She was tired and euphoric.

Susan talked to her for a while, making sure she was OK. 'Take your time, there's no hurry.'

She brought her some herbal tea, a chunk of bread and a pot of strawberry jam.

'You might not feel like it, but it would be good if you could have something to eat. I will leave you to rest for a while. Feel free to take a nap, there's a blanket on the sofa if you'd like. Give me a call if you need anything.' With that, Susan disappeared into the kitchen.

Germaine took a bite of the bread and the wonderfully sweet jam. She lay back on the sofa and within minutes she was fast asleep.

~ 30 ~

Driving back to London Germaine felt completely different. Tension she hadn't even been aware of in her shoulders and neck had been lifted. The content of the sessions with Susan seemed elusive, although her mind kept returning to a question Theo had asked her: 'What stops you from doing the things you love?'

As she sped through Hounslow, a large sign caught her attention, a picture of a golden Labrador puppy staring expectantly out at the viewer. She wasn't sure if it was the presence of a dog at Susan's place that had inspired her, but she had an overwhelming desire to have her own puppy.

When she arrived home, Ben was still out shopping. She grabbed the local paper and searched the personal ads section. She could feel the excitement build as she zeroed in on the words: '2 Labrador puppies for sale'.

The butterflies were loose in her stomach as she picked up the phone and dialled. A woman answered and Germaine quickly ascertained that both dogs were still available, one male and one female. The owner explained that potential buyers were coming in a couple of days' time to check them out and that she operated on a first come, first served basis.

Not wanting to risk losing out, Germaine booked an appointment for the following evening. She felt very excited, but also a little guilty about not talking it through with Ben first. She consoled herself with the fact that it was only a viewing, it wasn't a commitment.

At last Ben returned and Germaine greeted him with puppy-like enthusiasm. He found himself agreeing that getting a dog was a good idea. 'But how was the session? Is this what came out of it? Tell me about it,' he said.

'It was amazing. There was something spiritual about her. Not in a religious or woowoo way, very down to earth. You'd love her.'

'So did you work on your headaches, the scan?'

Ben had a way of shifting the tone of a conversation that on a good day would provoke amazing insights and great conversations, but on a bad day could lead to arguments and conflict. On this occasion Germaine withdrew a little to think. Finally, she answered, 'We talked about it, but the focus was more on me and my dad.'

She seemed to be testing the words for the familiar feelings they evoked, but found them without charge.

'It was a weird process and I do feel... different. Susan did say I will be still processing it, so I'm not sure about talking too much.'

The following evening Ben and Germaine went to Hounslow to meet their new dog. Germaine knew there was no way they'd be able to walk away from a puppy once they'd made the effort to go and see it. They were committed.

They parked outside the small terraced house where the dog breeder lived. Germaine rang the bell and expected to hear barking, but instead the door opened just a little and an eye appeared behind the opening.

'Hello?'

'We're looking for Jackie, the dog breeder.'

'Are you Germaine?'

'That's right.'

They heard a latch being released and the door opened more fully.

'Come in, dear. Is this your husband?'

'This is Ben, yes.' Germaine didn't know why, but she didn't want to say she wasn't married. 'It's not as if I'm adopting a baby,' she chided herself.

Jackie ushered them into the front room, where they took a seat and waited while she went off to fetch the puppies. She returned with one under each arm and put them down in the centre of the room. The slightly larger one came bounding over and sniffed Ben's shoes, then promptly sat on them. Ben and Germaine both laughed.

'That's that, then,' Ben said.

'He's the forward one, but he's pretty easy going.' Jackie smiled.

'Is there anything we need to know about him or puppies in general?' Germaine asked.

Jackie gave them a leaflet about looking after dogs and a certificate detailing the puppy's birth and pedigree. 'I've been calling him Barney but it's up to you to choose his real name.'

Ben looked at Germaine and smiled at the delight in her face. 'Barney works for me, what about you, Ger?'

'Yes, he looks like a little Barney.'

They walked out of the house with Barney in Ben's arms. The dog whimpered when he got in the car.

'You know, I didn't really expect to be coming home with him straight away. We haven't got anything for him, pet food, bedding, anything,' Ben said. 'I hope he doesn't wee on me.'

Germaine was so happy she didn't care what Barney did. 'Let's take him home and you can pop out and get a bed and his food.'

Ben could only smile back, pleased to see Germaine so happy.

~ 31 ~

Germaine had tried to arrange a face-to-face meeting with Theo, but the logistics just hadn't worked. She emailed him to tell him what had happened regarding work and her scan, and he suggested a telephone session.

'How are you now?' he asked when they began.

'Uh, better, and worse too,' she replied. She wasn't really sure.

Theo didn't respond, leaving a silence that Germaine felt compelled to fill.

'I'm up and down. I feel lighter, though, and some weird coincidences have been happening.'

'In my experience they aren't coincidences. I believe things happen to us and around us according to our consciousness. We make meaning out of things depending on what's on our mind.'

'Yes, that makes sense. One of those coincidences was around your friend Susan Watts. She popped up on three separate occasions, so I took it as a sign. I did a journey session with her that was really helpful. Maybe I've been feeling better because I've had a break from work. I don't know... I still feel emotional about stuff, but somehow more alive.'

'So what's going on for you right now?' Theo asked. The tone of his voice had an almost physical weight, focusing Germaine on the present.

'Good question. I've arranged another scan and a second opinion, which happens in three weeks. My consultant wanted me to have a biopsy, but I don't feel it's right. I'm shitting myself that I'm wrong and that the delay might kill me, but when I think of going under the knife my whole body reacts. I just don't know what to do.'

'I hear that you're in a tough place. You're afraid and there's a lot at stake. Here's the thing: people may give you advice, but it's your life, it's up to you whether you take their advice or not. If you don't mind, I'll reflect back what I see, purely with the intention of helping clarify things for you. Is that OK?'

Germaine realised she'd been secretly hoping Theo would wave a magic wand and make the decision for her, but now she understood that she'd had enough competing advice – if Theo had given her more it would only have added to her confusion.

'Clarity is what I want,' she said.

'Great. So as I understand it, your consultant wants you to have a biopsy immediately and you want to have another scan and a second opinion.'

'Yep, that's it.'

'The first thing I'd like to say is that fear can be very useful for information, but not necessarily for action. We don't know the result of our choices beyond the mundane and immediate response. For example, if you drop a cup from a height onto concrete, you pretty much know it will smash, although even then you can't guarantee it 100%. So all we can do really is make decisions on what we know and feel right now. Where are you at the moment, at home?'

'I'm in my bedroom, sitting on the end of the bed.'

'OK, can you stand up?'

'Yup, I have.'

'If you think of the worst-case scenario if you don't take the consultant's advice, what would that be?'

Taking a deep breath, Germaine let her thoughts follow the track of her worst fear and felt tears forming.

'That the tumour spreads and they have to remove more of my brain and that leaves me a vegetable.' She could feel something hardening inside her.

'How does that make you feel?'

'I hadn't spoken it out loud before. But you know, I've been through a lot recently and... I just don't believe it... it doesn't feel... real.'

'Interesting. You suddenly feel more present, is the word I would use. More substantial. Does that make sense to you?'

Germaine knew exactly what he meant, though she wouldn't have articulated it in those terms. She would have said she was becoming stronger, more resolved, more certain, like it was at the core of her.

'OK, let's give that scenario a name, say "Vegetable". Can you turn around on the spot and shake that worst-case scenario off?'

Germaine had done this before in a couple of Theo's sessions, so she jumped up and down and shook her arms, looking a little like an athlete limbering up for a sprint.

'Right,' said Theo, 'what's the best-case scenario if you don't take the first consultant's advice?'

Germaine thought for a moment. 'That the scan shows no tumour and I don't need any further treatment.'

'Great. How does that feel?'

Germaine had thought she would feel excited, but instead she felt normal. The steel in her core was still present. 'I feel good – grounded,' she said, then smiled. She was starting to sound like Theo.

'You sound grounded and I sense you're smiling. What's that about?'

'I guess it feels good not to be afraid,' she said.

'Great, so what shall we call this scenario?'

'"Grounded?"'

'If it represents how you feel here, it works for me. Now move over to a different part of the room. Is that possible?'

'Yes, it's a portable phone.' Germaine moved across the room to by the window.

'Right, the other option is to have the biopsy straight away. What's the worst that could happen?'

Germaine could feel tension building as she thought about going in for the surgery. Fear squeezed into the spaces between her organs, constricting her. 'That something goes wrong in surgery and I'm left handicapped, and then they find that the tumour was benign,' she said.

She paused. It was like a clarion call was sounding inside her. 'I should trust myself,' she realised. She felt a rush of emotion; it wasn't sadness or joy, but something in between.

'What are you feeling now?' Theo asked.

Germaine breathed slowly. She didn't want to speak. Having let her emotions settle, she finally spoke. 'How do you do that? That was... I didn't expect that... I got a strong hit about...' She had to pause again, as it felt like the steely core she had sensed earlier was pulsing with this emotion. Breathing deeply again, she said, 'Trust... trusting myself...'

Neither of them spoke for a while and that seemed completely right to Germaine. She felt wonderfully alive, fragile and incredibly strong at the same time.

'Remember this,' said Theo, breaking the silence. 'Though I suspect you won't forget it.'

'How does he know?' thought Germaine, but she stayed quiet.

'Just to clarify,' Theo continued, 'the worst case in going for the biopsy is that the tumour is benign, that the op goes wrong and that you didn't trust yourself. What shall we call this scenario?'

Germaine was still bathing in the afterglow of her experience and drew a blank.

'What about "No Trust"?' suggested Theo.

'I guess so,' Germaine agreed.

'Let's not get hung up on it. If something better occurs to you that's fine, but we can use it for now. OK, turn around again.'

Germaine turned and faced back into the room.

'What's the best-case scenario if you do go for the biopsy?'

'That they find the tumour and it's benign and they remove it and I'm fine.'

'How does that make you feel?'

'Strangely flat. Like it should make me feel good, but I feel it's irrelevant.'

'What do you want to call that one?'

'You know, it doesn't matter. I think I get the message.'

'So you're clear on what you're going to do?' Theo probed.

'For me it's about trusting myself. I know I don't want the biopsy now. It doesn't feel right. I am scared, but I have to accept that.'

'So what have you learned about yourself today?'

'That trust is really important to me. And that it's vital I trust myself.'

'Why's that so important?'

'It sets me free. I waste so much energy doubting myself, seeking approval that I don't accept anyway even if it comes. I have to accept and love myself.'

'And if you do love and accept yourself, what's available to you then?'

'If I accept and trust myself, I think my relationships will move to another level. I have good relationships, at home, with friends and at work, but I think if I'm more sure of myself I can be more honest and challenge things that don't work and I can be more myself.'

'And how might that help others?'

'It can only be a good thing for those around me. Some people might not like it, but it has to be that way for my sake.'

'There's a real conviction in your voice,' said Theo.

'You know, it's weird, but I feel like something tightened up in me, in a good way. Not stiff and brittle or suffocating like before, more like when you've done some exercise. I'm not explaining it very well.'

'I believe I know what you mean. It's similar to when you do Pilates or yoga and they talk about your "core" muscles. It sounds like you're feeling your emotional or perhaps spiritual core strengthening. What is possible for you when you feel like this?'

'Anything. I feel powerful, sure, like everything's OK. I just need to get out of my own way...'

She thought about herself, Mike, Jeremy and Dominic – how she shied away from confrontation and how they dominated the company, so that the likes of Tom didn't get the airtime they deserved. 'I realise now that I've lacked trust in myself,' she continued.

'And what do you feel is the impact of that on those around you?'

Germaine imagined dealing with herself. 'I guess they feel like they're left hanging, not sure of what I'm thinking and feeling or going to do.'

'Like your lack of trust in yourself creates a lack of trust of you in others?'

'Yes. It's like you said. My inner world creates my outer world.'

There was a pregnant silence. 'So what do you want?' Theo asked finally.

'To trust myself.'

'And what will that create in your world?'

'More trust.'

'You are the trust bringer,' Theo said.

Maybe it was the way he said it, but Germaine felt like something had been released. 'Yes. The trust bringer who builds relationships.' She felt a lump in her throat as she said it.

She wanted to laugh and cry at the same time, which is exactly what she did. 'I'm not even sure what that means, but it feels right at some deep level,' she continued.

'Say it again, Germaine,' Theo prompted.

'I am the trust bringer who builds relationships.' She felt like she was bubbling with energy and it needed to escape through laughter and crying.

'So what are you going to do differently, Germaine?' Theo asked.

'I am going to trust myself and my intuition. I will get a second opinion and another scan.'

'What else?'

'I'm not sure what you mean.'

'Well, if there's a gift that all this that's happening gives you, what might it be?'

'A gift?' Germaine was confused.

'In my experience our greatest challenges and hardships often bring us the greatest of gifts. If there was a gift in your current challenge, what might that be?'

The word came loud and clear into her mind. 'Forgiveness.'

'And what does that look like for you?'

'Forgiveness of my father... and of myself.' Germaine knew that was the healing she'd been crying out for, but this was the first time she'd stated it openly and with such clarity.

'Now that sounds like a pretty wonderful gift.' She could hear the smile in Theo's voice.

'You know, it's forgiveness full stop,' Germaine continued. 'Of myself, my father, my mum, Ben, old boyfriends, Sam, Mike, Jeremy – jeez, it's forgiving people I shouldn't need to forgive, but I do need to.'

She laughed. The pain of talking about her father had gone.

~ 32 ~

Germaine had two weeks until her appointment with the second specialist: two weeks to practise forgiveness, to follow her intuition.

She told Ben she was going to visit her dad's grave and he was surprised.

'Do you want me to come with you?'

'Actually no, it's something I want to do on my own,' Germaine replied. On a whim, she grabbed the phone and dialled. 'Just calling Mum.'

Ben raised his eyebrows in surprise and went off to the kitchen to make himself a drink.

The phone was answered on the fourth ring. 'Hello?' said a quiet voice.

'She's old,' thought Germaine and a well of compassion surged in her heart. 'How you doing, Mum?'

"Oh, hello, darling. There's nothing wrong, is there?'

'No,' said Germaine, thinking she should have thought this through a bit more. 'I've got some time off work and I wanted to see you.' She hadn't intended to say that, but realised she could go to see her mother on the way to her father's grave.

'That would be nice,' her mum replied. 'I was just thinking about going to bed, I've been out in the garden most of the day cutting the roses back and sorting the shed. Working in the fresh air always makes me a bit sleepy. Geoff's been helping me.'

'Who's Geoff?' Germaine asked, surprised.

'Geoff Burns, from the garden centre. You met him last year.'

'Did I?'

'Yes, I introduced you. Anyway, when are you thinking of coming? You're welcome any time. Will Ben be coming too?'

'No, it's just me. Are you around tomorrow afternoon?'

'Yes, that's fine. I've got to pick up a parcel in the morning, but I'm free in the afternoon. What a lovely surprise. Will you be here for lunch and tea?'

'Umm, let's see. It would be lovely to see you for lunch, let me take you out. But I can't stay for tea, I need to get back.'

'Oh, that would be lovely. I could book The Naked Meal, it's an organic restaurant that opened last month.'

Germaine was a little surprised – her mum hadn't been the sort to eat out often. 'I was actually thinking of going to Dad's grave,' she said in a rush.

There was silence. After what seemed an age, her mum replied, 'That's a good idea, Germaine. Do you know where it is?'

'You know I don't. You can tell me tomorrow.'

'You don't want me to come, do you?'

'I don't think so, no,' said Germaine, wondering if her mother was relieved at that.

~ 33 ~

The drive out to her mum's house the following morning was a road she'd travelled many times, but things looked different to her. Was it really that long since she'd been to visit her?

As she walked up the path to the semi-detached house, she noticed that the fences and front door had been recently painted. She pressed the buzzer and was immediately greeted by her mum, who looked younger, more alive than she'd been for the last few years.

'You been out shopping, Mum?' Germaine asked. 'You've upgraded yourself.'

'Cheeky monkey,' said her mum, but she looked pleased. 'You look lovely too, darling. Come on in. We can have a quick cup of tea. I booked a table for 12. I know it's a bit early, but we were lucky to get that, they're so busy.'

The house was different inside, too: it was less cluttered and the walls had been stripped of the tired wallpaper and instead painted a simple off-white.

'Wow, Mum, you have been busy.'

'No point wallowing in the past,' her mum replied. 'And it was about time.'

'So what's been going on?'

Her mum suddenly looked like a young girl. 'We'll talk over lunch. I'm going to get some tea and I want to hear all about you.'

Germaine followed her to the kitchen, leaving her bag by the door as she had done a thousand times. The kitchen was the same as always. She sat at the table while her mother brought the cups and pot over on a tray. Her mum's hands were like butterflies flitting between objects, making sure they were just so. Her blue-grey eyes looked bright with intelligence. Germaine felt a welling of love for her.

'It's really nice to see you, Mum,' Germaine said and she meant it. 'I'm sorry I haven't been there for you. I've been wrapped up in my own stuff.'

'Germaine, I know you're busy – you've got to live your own life. You shouldn't have to worry about your mum. I'm fine, really. I would love to see you more and I do worry about you, but I know you'd come to me if you needed anything.' She put her hand on Germaine's in a spontaneous show of motherly concern. 'Is everything OK with you and Ben? How come you're off work?'

The light, cool touch of her hand and its silky smoothness drew Germaine back to the present. 'Everything's fine with Ben. We have our ups and downs, but we're pretty good together. I have got some time off from work, though.'

She'd been thinking of protecting her mum from the truth, but looking into her eyes she knew she had to tell her what was happening. 'The thing is, I'd been having dizzy spells so I went for some tests. Something showed up on a scan of my brain, but we're not sure what it is. I need to have more tests.'

Her mum looked shocked and then, once she'd gathered herself, concerned.

'When do you find out?' asked her mum, caressing Germaine's hand.

Thinking back, her mum had always been the pragmatic one; in times of crisis she'd managed to hold things together. She may have been timid and quiet, but she was also balanced and practical.

'I only found out a few days ago, but really there's nothing to worry about,' Germaine reassured her.

'Of course I'm worried. I know you'll handle it, darling, but I'm your mum and I'm allowed to worry. Are you sure you want to go for lunch?'

'Yes, of course, I'm looking forward to it. You did such a good sell on the place. Shall we go in my car?'

Germaine really liked the restaurant. They'd opted for a shabby chic look, with chunky wooden furniture, plenty of light, vibrant art and large farmhouse cutlery and plates. The menu looked great, but she and her mum only ordered a light lunch.

From their smalltalk about what they'd both been up to, Germaine gleaned that some of her mum's new-found energy originated in a man.

'It's Geoff, isn't it?'

'Now, Germaine, there's nothing to it. We're taking it slowly, we have the same circle of friends and we're just enjoying each other's company.' Her mum flushed slightly as she spoke and changed the subject. 'Anyway, what's this about wanting to see your dad's grave after all this time?'

'I know it sounds a bit weird, but I think it's necessary. I've started to clean up my act, change my thinking and look at my life differently. I just think it's time... time to put that ghost to bed. I think going to his grave will give me some closure.'

'You know it's the anniversary of his death today, don't you?'

Germaine's stomach dropped. 'No, I had no idea.'

'Yes, it's exactly ten years ago. For the first few years after his death I visited his grave, but then I stopped. Strangely enough, I did go last week. He wasn't a bad man, you know. We had a lot of fun together. He just lost his way a bit. I don't think things worked out the way he wanted them to and he got frustrated.'

Germaine was curious. She couldn't believe she hadn't talked to her mum about her father since he died.

'What actually happened the day you told me you were separating?' she asked.

'That was one of the worst days of my life.' Her mum looked sad. 'I found it hard to forgive him for that. I wanted to let you find out gently, but he thought you were old enough and deserved to know the truth. He said you were a strong cookie and knew your own mind.'

'I was never quite good enough for him,' said Germaine.

'Oh, that's so not true, darling. He was hard on you, I know, like he was on himself. He wanted you to be more than he was, to get what you wanted in life. To be honest, I think he was depressed for a long time; I simply didn't like to face up to it. He loved you, he just wasn't so good at showing it. In the end we drifted apart and he found someone who could listen and help. I don't think it worked in the end, but for a while he definitely was happier.'

She was about to say more, but their food arrived. Halfway through the meal, Germaine noticed her mum was smiling to herself. 'What are you thinking, Mum?'

'I just remembered the first dinner out your dad and I had after you were born. You were three, I think, and Nan had agreed to look after you. We didn't have much money and it was a rare treat to go out for dinner at all, but we went to a lovely little restaurant by the river. I hadn't been drinking for a while and being so tired I practically drifted off at the table. Your dad fell about laughing. It's a silly story, really, but the look in your eyes reminded me.'

A small tear appeared at the corner of her eye and Germaine felt a rush of emotion. She grabbed her mum's hand, but was lost for words.

'I think it's good that you're going to his grave,' her mum went on. 'It's taken me a long time to be able to remember your dad without the hurt. You know, we both loved you. The only times I saw him cry were over you. At your birth, then once when he hit you when you were little – he hated himself for that – and then when he told you we were separating. He tried to do the right thing by you, but he always felt he was failing you.'

Germaine was conscious this was probably the first time she had talked with her mum on a grown-up level. 'I love you, Mum. I don't think I've told you that enough,' she said.

'I love you too, darling. As a family we don't talk much about our feelings.'

At the end of their meal Germaine felt more connected to her mum than she could remember ever feeling as an adult.

Her mum handed her a piece of paper. 'I wrote some directions. The grave is a devil to find and I didn't want to try to explain it. Are you sure you don't want to come back to mine after you've been there?'

'No, Mum, but it's been really nice to catch up and perhaps you can come and stay with us for a weekend soon.'

They hugged and Germaine held on just a little longer than usual.

~ 34 ~

Germaine drove through the gates of the cemetery. The stone archway over the entrance looked cold and lifeless.

She parked the car and stepped onto the gravel. The stones grinding underfoot produced a strangely evocative sound. She felt the cool air on her skin and her heartbeat was insistent in its slow, pounding rhythm. She pulled out the directions her mum had given her and became acutely aware of the crisp white paper contrasting starkly with the wet greyness around her.

Germaine wandered up the path, her feet heavy, not really taking in the directions but feeling guided somehow. She realised she hadn't been breathing when she could hardly take a step more. She slumped on a shiny marble grave, her head and heart pounding. She knew somehow that her head was between her legs.

'I hope I don't go over.' The thought pierced the void she was feeling.

She came to, the icy-cold marble against her back. The greyness had been replaced by the pink veil that was her eyelid. Her eyes opened to a bright winter sky, a pigeon flying high on a mission. She felt a flush of well-being incongruous with her situation.

Sitting up, she looked around to see if anyone had witnessed her passing out, but she was alone with the dead.

'What's going on, Germaine?' she said out loud and felt a little silly. 'Talking to yourself in a graveyard, that's pretty weird.' She started to laugh.

That felt good and she laughed harder, aware that she must look completely mad. When her stomach ached and her chest felt like it could take no more, she stopped. Her eye was drawn to a splash of yellow among the headstones. She got up to look.

The gold lettering read:

Edward Michael Willis
Born 30th January 1952
Died 9th November 2003

Was that it, was that the sum of it all? You were here and now you're not.

She stood silently, remembering things from her childhood, both good and bad, until she started to ache.

'I forgive you, Dad.' Just like that, the words came out. They sounded strange. 'I forgive you and I love you. I'm sorry that I didn't really get to know you. I didn't understand you... but I forgive you.'

She placed her hand on the stone. 'Goodbye, Dad.' A tear drop smashed against the black marble. Germaine took a deep breath, pulled her jacket closed against the cold and returned to her car to drive home.

~ 35 ~

When she met Dr Bron for her second opinion she liked him. He came across as slightly arrogant, but she guessed that went with the territory. People had to trust his decisions and they were often life-or-death ones. His eyes and voice were gentle and careworn and she had no doubt that he had a kind heart. Germaine described exactly her fainting episodes and what had led up to them.

'Have you had any more fainting episodes since your initial scan?'

'Just one and I think that might have been more circumstantial.'

His eyebrows remained elevated, inviting her to elaborate.

'I was in a particularly emotional state and was out of breath.'

'Ah, I see. When was the last one?'

'About two weeks ago.'

He concurred with the original prognosis, but in the light of Germaine's insistence and to allay her fears he agreed to a second scan.

She noticed he had a habit of rotating his fountain pen in his right hand when contemplating what to say. His bushy grey eyebrows rose dramatically when he finished a sentence.

On a whim, she called Sam. Germaine realised she'd been avoiding her friend, but wanted to tell her what had been going on. She'd not returned a number of Sam's calls and emails and had definitely distanced herself, but she'd rationalised it as being so she could focus on getting well.

When she told Ben she was planning to meet Sam, he asked how her friend was, and she could feel jealousy raising its ugly head.

Ben and she had been getting on so well. He'd been a rock for her, his calm and sensitivity a safe harbour in all the turmoil. But mentioning Sam had reminded her of the arguments before her initial diagnosis. She hadn't trusted the two of them. They'd stayed out together that night and she'd felt betrayed. Logically the idea was absurd, but the serpent started to uncoil again.

'What's up? You look like you're chewing a wasp,' asked Ben, cocking his head – a pose he'd adopted from Barney.

'What happened that night we were supposed to go to the cinema and I didn't make it?' Germaine asked. 'You and Sam went on somewhere.'

Ben looked confused and surprised. 'Umm, I don't remember exactly. We saw the film and then went to a couple of bars, no idea what they were called. Why, what's this about?'

She thought he looked sheepish, a bit shifty. 'I've talked to you about trust and how important it is to me. I've been feeling resentful towards Sam and I think it's to do with you. Did anything happen between you two?'

'Of course not,' said Ben with conviction, but immediately afterwards there was a betraying flicker in his eyes.

'You're not being straight with me,' Germaine accused him.

'Did Sam say something?'

'The bastard, he's looking defensive,' thought Germaine and could feel her hackles rising. 'What would she have to say, Ben?' she asked, ice in her voice.

'Nothing, don't get so worked up. We just talked. I was offloading, it didn't mean anything.'

'What didn't mean anything?'

'As I said, I was just offloading. I told her you were difficult to live with. I didn't know the whole story of what you were going through, I thought you were finding it hard adjusting to us living together. I confided in Sam that I was considering moving out to give you and me more space.'

Germaine felt like someone had knocked the wind out of her. Her anger and indignation had been snuffed out.

'I didn't realise,' she said, feeling both ashamed and relieved.

'It's all fine,' he said. 'I understand now that it was all the pressure at work... and stuff about your dad. But we're through it. I couldn't be happier now. You can trust me. I didn't want to say anything then because Sam put me straight and I'd just needed to vent a bit. I am disappointed she mentioned it now, though.'

'She didn't. I'm sorry for doubting you and I've got some apologising to do to Sam, too.'

That night Ben didn't know what had hit him. Germaine's inner strength had translated into sexual aggression and he wasn't complaining.

'What's got into you?' he said, smiling and lying back on the pillow.

Germaine giggled. 'I'm not getting enough! No... It's just I'm feeling really alive.'

Ben's smile froze briefly. She suddenly realised the impact her health issues must be having on him.

'You don't have to worry, I know it's going to be fine,' she said. 'I don't know how I know, but I do. You don't know what the future may bring and you can't change the past, so why worry about it?'

What would it be like to live like this all the time?

~ 36 ~

By the time Germaine went for her second scan she felt great. It seemed like she had ditched a backpack full of emotional baggage and was floating on a wave of positivity. She knew that whatever the results were, she would be OK.

After the scan, she decided she wanted to go to Dr Bron's office on her own. He was all smiles.

'How are you feeling, Germaine?'

'Fantastic, thank you.'

It was bizarre to be feeling this good while awaiting news of this magnitude. She just wanted him to get on with it.

'I'm sure you're anxious to know the results of the scan,' he said, 'and in fact I'm glad you came to me for a second opinion. The scan shows that the tumour is smaller than it first appeared, as you can see.' He showed Germaine the original scan and then the second one.

'Are you saying that it's going?' she asked.

'I can't say that, I'm afraid, but what I am saying is it appears smaller than on the original scan. The tumour is discrete and sits just outside of the brain itself so it's most likely a type of tumour called a meningioma. It may not seem like it, but you're lucky. If you're going to have a tumour, this is probably the one to have. The likelihood is that it's benign.'

Germaine felt a warm glow and wanted to go and tell Ben the news. 'So it's not cancer. Thank you, doctor.'

'It would appear not. It is still a serious condition, as it puts pressure on the brain.' His eyebrows danced as he considered how to phrase his next sentence. 'In this case it would appear to be a very slow-growing one, though. You have two options: leave it be and have regular check-ups, or operate and remove the tumour now.'

'What would you do if it were you?' asked Germaine, thinking it was strange that she was not getting her previous reaction to the idea of surgery.

'Without a doubt, given the type, size and location I'd have the operation, as that would give me the greatest sense of security. You'd still need regular check-ups afterwards, but the prognosis would be very favourable.'

'When would I have to decide?'

'As I said, it's slow growing, so take some time... it's your life and it's a big decision. There are of course risks involved in any surgery. Talk it through with your family. It's also worthwhile talking to patients who've had the surgery and those who decided not to. There's information about support groups in this leaflet and much more on the web, but be discerning.'

For the next few days Germaine spent a lot of time researching, talking to other people and soul searching. Ben was her sounding board. He had his own views, but tried hard not to impose them.

'It's up to me,' she kept saying to herself, all the time remembering what Theo had said.

She read her journal again and was surprised how far she had come. When she revisited the wheel of life she'd filled in at the beginning, she realised everything had changed. How bizarre that in what was probably the most traumatic time of her life she actually felt more healthy – more balanced, more grounded and more purposeful. Life was strange.

She decided to go on a bike ride and set off along the river towards Richmond Park, Barney running alongside her. The sun was streaming through the clouds. It had rained in the morning, but the forecast was good for the rest of the day.

The constant exertion was therapeutic. By the time they had climbed Richmond Hill and hit the middle of the park, Germaine was breathing hard and so was Barney. There were very few people around and Barney busied himself sniffing at various animal leavings, ravenously hoovering up a couple of nuggets. Germaine nearly gagged, but then she laughed. He was blissfully oblivious to his faux pas. 'I guess when it comes down to it, it really does depend on your point of view,' she thought. 'It's poo to us, but to him it's just stuff with something in it that smells good enough to eat.'

She found a fallen log beneath a large oak tree, laid her bike down and checked that the log was suitable to sit on. The light dappled through the branches and she remembered her safe place from her journey work with Susan. Barney suddenly barked and rushed off, tail wagging, chasing away a chattering squirrel. Germaine breathed deeply, letting the air fill her lungs.

On a whim, she took off her trainers and socks and put her feet on the damp, mossy grass. It felt really good. There was something primal about it.

Sam had said she should have the operation and had put her in touch with a friend of hers who had had a tumour removed from his head a number of years ago. For him it had all been about the peace of mind. Peace of mind for a piece of mind – that was almost amusing.

Ben, on the other hand, thought she should try the self-healing route for a while. When Germaine checked what she thought about that she felt tight, like something wasn't moving.

She realised that she was afraid. She was afraid of dying, of making the wrong choices and of how she would look if she did have the operation. While the idea of having a metal plate in her head was a little freaky, she had been hugely relieved that she wouldn't need chemo and that the surgery would be easily disguised in her hairline.

So what the hell was she going to do?

On a whim she picked up a cone. 'This represents leaving the tumour alone,' she thought. Then she picked up a feather, which represented having an operation. Interesting.

She looked at the pine cone. It was tightly packed and its scales were inseparable ridges, keeping their bounty from the elements. It was hard and unyielding.

Then she turned to the feather in her left hand. It was white with a few brown flecks at the edges. A thing of beauty, it was light and almost irrelevant. It didn't matter. Something struck a chord with her, although she wasn't quite sure what it was.

After sitting for a while weighing the two objects in her hand, she felt a little clearer. 'Trust yourself, Germaine,' she thought. It was her choice, her life. She had nothing to prove to anyone, not even herself.

~ 37 ~

The night before her operation, neither Germaine nor Ben found it easy to sleep. They talked about the things they'd done together, listened to a couple of guided meditations and talked about what they wanted for the future.

When Germaine finally drifted into sleep, she dreamed of a black, hard, conical shape. It radiated cold through her, leaving her numb and almost paralysed. Her heart laboured at the pressure of the cold. She was under water, the dark depths all around her. Her lungs screamed to let go of the dead air within, her head pounded at the beat of her straining heart. 'I don't want to die!' she heard herself screaming. She could hold on no longer. She let go and allowed the blackness in. 'I am the darkness, nothingness,' she thought.

Then she could see a point of light in the darkness, although it was really small. If she could just focus on the point she'd be OK. Her eyes strained to focus – there it was, there. Her pupils dilated to their limit and she thought she had it... then it overwhelmed her. She was drifting in a sea of light and she felt euphoric.

When she woke up she remembered the dream and she was calm. It had left her feeling held, knowing that everything would be OK, whatever happened.

When the time came to be anaesthetised, she gave Ben a hug and they told each other they'd be fine. The whole episode felt surreal. She was displaced from herself, observing her own behaviour. Counting backwards she almost laughed: going down the steps to my safe place... here we go again... just like fainting... and...

The next she knew she was sitting up in bed with various tubes attached and she could see Dr Bron's smiling face, his eyebrows a pair of bushy arches to his twinkly eyes.

'How are you feeling, Germaine?'

Luckily she couldn't speak at first as her mouth was parched, or she might have said that was a silly question. She worked saliva into her mouth and realised that despite the grogginess she didn't feel too bad, not like she would expect after having major surgery. She could feel some less than jaunty headwear, though, and thought she must look a state.

'Can I have a mirror?' she asked.

From behind Dr Bron Ben's voice said, 'Typical, she wants to put on her make-up.'

'Germaine, the operation was textbook, no complications,' the doctor told her. 'We'll obviously need to keep you in for observation, but I don't see why you couldn't be back home in a day or so. The tumour was beautifully discrete and the tissue of the brain was unaffected.'

'But how do I look?' was all she could say.

'You're understandably a bit swollen and you've got a bit of a turban on, but I explained to Ben that we didn't require a plate and we wired the bone flap back into place. You still need to be mindful of X-rays though,' said Dr Bron.

'You're a sight for sore eyes,' Ben said warmly.

~ 38 ~

It was a little strange returning to work: incredibly familiar yet subtly different, as if memory and reality were competing for precedence. Perhaps she was seeing the changes in the place or maybe she herself had changed and saw things differently.

Germaine checked her feelings as she entered the main office. She felt glad to be back, but a little nervous. That wasn't helped by the memory of the conversation she had had with Jeremy before her return. He'd seemed surprised at first, then genuinely pleased. He'd told her a lot had happened while she was away, some of it pretty major, but he'd talk to her about it when she came in.

She had started to worry about what those changes were and how they might be related to her. She noticed she was getting into a familiar pattern of anxiety, and she chose to let it go. After what she'd just been through, nothing could really be that important. That was easy to do at home, but back in the office it was a totally different kettle of fish.

When Katherine saw Germaine she immediately jumped up from her chair, rushed over and gave her a big hug. Owen came towards her too, smiling.

'You're back!' Katherine beamed.

'We've missed you,' said Owen with touching warmth.

In that moment Germaine felt a glow of affection for her team. 'Are you guys free later this morning for a catch-up?' she asked.

'I've got an 11 o'clock, but everything else can be shifted around,' Katherine offered.

Owen nodded. 'I left today pretty flexible when Jeremy said you would be in. There's lots to talk about.'

'Yep, I've got to see Jeremy first. Is he in yet?'

'Not sure. He's been out a lot recently. Mike's been in control.' Katherine emphasised the world 'control' in a telling manner.

'Sorry, we haven't let your feet touch the ground before bombarding you with...'

Owen was cut off by a voice projected from behind Germaine. 'There she is! How the devil are you?'

Dominic strode over and enveloped Germaine in a big hug. 'You look fantastic. Are you sure you've been ill, not chilling out in a spa somewhere?'

Katherine and Owen looked concerned at the insensitivity, but Germaine laughed. 'At least some things never change,' she said, tapping Dominic playfully on the chest.

'Ah, you've heard, eh? We should chat.' Dominic gave a flick of the eyes towards Katherine and Owen before adding, 'Must dash now, but let me know when you're free. Chloe's got my diary. Or what are you doing tonight?'

Germaine was confused. 'What have I heard? I'm not getting sucked straight in,' she thought. She momentarily debated lying and saying she had something on, but instead found herself saying, 'Tonight doesn't work for me, but I will see you later.' She wondered why Chloe was looking after him now, but didn't say anything.

'OK, now I need half an hour with my emails, so if you'll all excuse me,' she said and went to her desk.

When sifting through emails over the last few days she'd noticed that the volume had markedly reduced over time. She'd concluded her team had consciously stopped copying her in on standard info emails, although the odd email that she was included on had let her know things hadn't totally fallen apart in her absence.

'It's good to be back,' she said to herself and meant it, despite being slightly overwhelmed. She tapped her keyboard and revealed something on her screen that made her cry. It was a picture of her team and the message: 'We're glad you're back. We missed you.'

When she looked up, through the tears she saw that all her team were looking over and smiling broadly. She was speechless.

'What are they thinking of, making you cry on your first day?' Tom was leaning over the partition. 'Welcome back. The place has been weird without you!'

~ 39 ~

Just as Germaine was starting to feel she was settling back into her job, Jeremy arrived. She caught his eye as soon as he entered the office. He looked tired, but his face lit up with a tangle of emotions when he saw her.

'Germaine, you look great,' he said. 'You busy right now?'

'Nothing that can't wait.'

'Great. Let's grab a coffee and sit down. Lots to talk about.'

When she joined him in his office, he seemed to be scrabbling around in his mind for the right words. 'So it wasn't cancer then. What were they doing putting you through all that? It must have been hell. We've been worried sick about you.'

Germaine was touched by his concern. 'I want to thank you again, Jeremy. You were so supportive.' As she said it a lump came to her throat. 'I know you don't like this sort of thing, but thank you.'

Jeremy looked embarrassed. 'Just glad you're OK. The time off has done you a world of good. You look really well.'

'Maybe you could do with a bit of time off yourself – you look tired,' she said. 'What's going on?'

'Well, I wasn't sure what I should say to you given your condition...' he began.

'I'm fine. I haven't felt this well for ages, so don't worry about me. What's going on? You've sold the company, haven't you?' She spoke the words before her brain had registered what she was saying.

Jeremy looked up, holding her gaze. 'Yes, who told you?'

'No one. It just occurred to me that was what must have happened.' Germaine realised she hadn't got that sinking feeling in her stomach that usually accompanied news of this sort. 'What's going to happen to the business? Who's buying us?'

'It's kind of complicated, but we're going to be part of a bigger agency. I didn't want you to hear it second hand and I really didn't want to tell you over the phone.'

'Who else knows?'

'Just Mike and Dominic as far as I'm aware... and Chloe, of course. They're under strict instructions not to tell anyone until we have all our ducks in a row.'

'So what happens now? Do I take it the details haven't been finalised?'

'There are conditions, but largely it's down to us, we get to shape it. It's a good move. They want to ensure they keep key personnel and they'll make it pretty lucrative to do so. I had to assure them I would stay on. We need to flesh out the details on how we will integrate, but the most immediate concern is identifying who we consider to be key personnel and what they will do. You and Dominic were singled out as part of their due diligence.'

Germaine couldn't help but feel relieved, although at the same time she felt a tightening in her stomach. It was like the old 'Am I good enough?' feeling, which she really needed to let go of.

'What about Mike and Tom?' Germaine asked.

'Mike's done what he was there for and I'm not sure what action he wants to take now. He's playing his cards close to his chest. Tom is Tom and will do whatever he's told,' said Jeremy.

'I'm sure he'd love to hear you say that,' she thought, but said out loud, 'I get the feeling you're not being totally up front with me. What are you not saying?'

Jeremy looked uncomfortable. 'The board... no, let's rewind. You know I think you're great. Especially with the coaching, I've seen you grow in confidence and stature. I even talked to Theo to see whether you were up for taking on a more senior role. I will be honest, I saw you as my ideal replacement... and then you got ill.'

Germaine wasn't sure she liked the thought of Jeremy and Theo discussing her.

Jeremy must have seen the look on her face. 'Don't worry, Theo wouldn't say anything to me. But you see, I was in a quandary. Alistair thought you were great and could see you fitting into their culture perfectly. You made a real impression the night we all met, and to be honest I think that might have had a big part to play in getting the deal on the table. As part of the acquisition I'm staying on to keep things ticking over here, but I've also got more of an integration role plus a few other little projects I want to get off the ground. I know it's a lot to take in and I'm sorry to do it on your first day back, but I'd like you to have a think about what you want to do. Feel free to take the rest of the day off to think about it if that's what you need.'

Talk about hitting the ground running.

~ 40 ~

Germaine was feeling exhausted and it wasn't even lunchtime. Back at her desk, she had an overwhelming urge to contact Theo. She wrote a quick email:

> Hi Theo,
> Hope all well.
> Just to let you know I ended up having surgery and all went well. I am back at work now and feeling better than I have done in years. Who would have thought?
> I feel like I have somehow been given a new lease of life and I'm determined to make the most of it.
> Thanks so much for your presence and guidance. It has been so inspiring and enlightening working with you. It couldn't have come at a better time.
> I'm conscious we didn't book our next session and was wondering if you had any availability this week or if not, next week?
> G

Having sent the email, she remembered she was supposed to be sitting down with Owen and Katherine. She spotted Liam coming from the kitchen with a coffee in his hand and wondered how he'd been doing since his father died.

'Hi, Liam, you got a minute?'

'Hey, Germaine, how are you?' He had genuine concern on his face.

'Fine, although it's been a frantic reintroduction. How have you been? Do you want to ditch that and get a proper coffee?'

Liam looked a little surprised. 'OK, sure.'

'Great. Just give me a minute, I need to reschedule a meeting.' Then she thought and called across the room, 'Owen, Katherine, it's 11:45. Do you fancy an early lunch? Let's go to the pub with Liam and you can all fill me in on what's been happening.'

Returning just over an hour later, Germaine felt a lovely sense of pride. Her team had not just managed but had made great progress in a couple of important accounts and there had been dramas but no disasters. Liam seemed to have developed a stronger relationship with Owen; reading between the lines she could tell that Owen had been unobtrusively lending him a guiding hand.

Remembering what Theo had talked about regarding feedback, she said, 'Guys, I'd like to thank you. You all really stepped up. I couldn't be more proud and grateful to have you as a team.'

Back at her desk, she saw she had an email from Mike with the subject line 'Meeting':

> Hi Germaine
> I heard you're in today. Are you available for a chat this afternoon at 2:30 or 4 pm for 30 mins?
> Mike

She wondered what the old dog was up to, and emailed him back:

> 2:30 is fine. Any context to the meeting? Just a catch-up?
> G

Two minutes later she got a text in response: 'Just a chat, don't worry.'

Wondering why she should worry, she saw that an email had just popped in from Theo:

> Hi Germaine
> Fantastic news. I was wondering ;-) Hoping you're making sure you don't overload :-)
> I can do 45 minutes tonight at 8 pm or it will have to be in 3 weeks as I will be incommunicado for a while. Let me know.
> Theo

Tonight seemed a bit desperate, but three weeks? What was that about?

When Mike arrived he looked like a man on a mission. Jenny, the office manager, was trailing in his wake. Her slight figure and the way she orbited Mike, struggling to keep up, put Germaine in mind of a seagull flapping for scraps around a trawler. The image brought a smile to her face.

When he caught sight of Germaine Mike stopped. 'You OK with that, Jenny? We can sort the rest out later,' he said, dismissing her. Then he added, smiling at Germaine, 'Back in the thick of it? We can talk now if you're free.'

After he'd closed the door of the conference room he wasted little time on pleasantries. 'I guess Jeremy has talked to you.'

'About the takeover?'

'Well, it's not a takeover, it's a sale. We chose to sell – in fact, we courted it.' The way he said it put Germaine in her place. 'It's about money, Germaine. That's what business is all about. I know that's not your strong point.'

Germaine felt her stomach tense, as if preparing for a physical blow.

'So I thought I might help you,' Mike continued. 'The company is going to make it worthwhile for certain employees to stay on through the transition. We're in a good bargaining position. As the client services director you are in a key role and I can help you negotiate a good package. I think I could get you an extra 30% on your salary plus better bonuses.'

She calculated what that meant and felt like a kid in a sweet shop. But with that feeling came another, as if she'd been caught with her hand in the jar. She knew she was being manipulated, but couldn't work out how or why.

'Thanks, Mike, that's kind and I appreciate the offer. But it's all a lot to take in at the moment and I will have to think about it.'

Mike looked a little confused. 'Don't take too long, there are some ambitious people here. Those who act quickly in times of instability are the ones who get ahead. And we don't want the decision made for us. You're valuable at the moment and you should make use of that fact. I have plenty of experience in this, I know how to make it happen.'

What was he talking about? He didn't seem to be referring only to negotiating her salary. She felt drained and deflated, despite the apparent bounty on offer.

Back at her desk, she sat down heavily. Remembering the metaphor Theo had told her about the bridge, she replied to his email:

Hi Theo
Tonight would be perfect. I'm in need of a bit of support. I'm feeling the pressure about a decision I need to make.
G

~ 41 ~

Ben had taken Barney for an evening sniff around the streets. Germaine had a sneaking suspicion he used dog walking as an excuse for a quick pint, and indeed Barney did seem to have an unusual attraction to pubs. She took the opportunity to grab the phone and dialled Theo's number.

'Theo speaking.' His voice was calm and relaxed.

'Hi, Theo, it's Germaine. Thanks for agreeing to speak to me tonight.'

'That's fine, Germaine, it suits me too. I'm curious about what's going on. How are you?'

'I feel well, incredible really after everything I've been through. I guess part of me feels so blessed to have been able to come out the other side.'

'That's really great to hear. You're a strong and resilient woman and I have no doubt you'll be an inspiration to others. So tell me what it's like being back at work.'

'Well, that's what I wanted coaching on. You see, I've got a decision to make and I want to trust my intuition, but I'm not clear about it. I've been going round and round in circles. Even talking about it again now makes me feel like I'm in turmoil, and I know you said my state is the most important thing when making important decisions.'

Germaine paused, realising she'd been talking without taking a breath. Theo remained silent for a few seconds.

'Are you still there?' she asked.

'Yes.'

'Well, what do you think?'

'You told me you have a decision to make but you're not in the right state, am I correct?'

'Yes.'

'So what is the right state?'

'Grounded and able to listen to my intuition, but I feel overwhelmed.'

'So what do you know about your state?'

'That I'm creating it through my thoughts. I know... When I'm at home and talking to Ben I can change perspective and I do feel differently, but as soon as I start thinking about the situation I get drawn back into the same state.'

'Great, so you can use perspective, but you're finding that you're more attached to the current perspective and it's more compelling for some reason. So we could look at finding a more compelling perspective or alternatively think about other tools you have.'

'Yes, of course, the EFT. I've been doing it, but I keep forgetting about it.'

'OK, let's give that a try. Thinking about the decision you have to make, what comes up?'

She tapped out the emotions and up came the conversation she had had with Mike earlier that day. She realised that the issue was still about trust. She knew that Mike was not being straight and was manipulating her, but also that she still wasn't trusting herself enough.

'You sound more grounded when you talk now,' Theo fed back to her when she told him the situation with the sale of the agency.

'Yes, I guess I feel it, but I still don't know what to do.'

'I have to say something at this point. Jeremy did talk to me about you and ask whether I thought you would be interested or even in a fit state to take on the MD role. Of course, I couldn't offer an opinion, but I did encourage him to talk to you. However, I also said I would encourage you to talk to him. On reflection, I shouldn't have committed to asking you to do that. It's outside the scope of the coaching and as such I apologise.'

Even though Germaine had known about the conversation, she felt a mix of emotions: disappointment and relief, but above all a sense of something clicking into place. 'Thanks for telling me, Theo,' she said.

'Don't be too hard on yourself. You've been through a lot recently and even without all these major changes happening, the adjustment involved in getting back to work was going to be tough. You've dealt with it all amazingly and I'm proud and inspired by the person you've become.'

Germaine could feel pride in herself blossoming. It was as if Theo had shone a light on something hidden, something she wasn't aware was there.

'I am proud of myself,' she said. There it was: no self-judgement, no sense it was wrong to feel that way.

Theo continued, 'In times of uncertainty it's good to look at your purpose and your vision, what you want for yourself and for others. Remind me what your vision is.'

'To have balance in my life. To be a role model for women and create a working environment where tremendous success doesn't come at the cost of individuals' health and personal growth. To have a family and a successful career.'

'Great, and what's your purpose?'

'The trust bringer who builds relationships.'

'Excellent. So how can those inform your decision?' Theo left the question hanging. 'With your vision in mind, what do you think your choices are?'

'There are two choices plus a side one Mike has added. Shall I include that one?'

'Do you want to?'

'Umm, yes, I think so. OK, the choices are to stay on as client services director; to stay on as client services director with Mike's help to get a better package; to start looking elsewhere for a similar role, although I know I don't want to do that; or to take on a more senior role, which would be MD, I guess.'

When she said that out loud it was like someone had let loose a net of eels in her stomach.

'What are you feeling right now?' Theo asked.

'How does he do that?' she thought, but said, 'Nervous, like who do I think I am? I'm not qualified.'

'Let's initially put the first two into one option, to stay in your current role. How would staying in your current role move you towards your vision?' Theo asked.

'Umm, I don't think it does. It seems like the safe option.'

'When you think of doing that, how do you feel?'

'I'd be disappointed. It's like everything's changing and I want some stability, but I would actually be going backwards, missing an opportunity.'

'I'm getting an image of you on an ice field that is breaking up all around you and you're scared to get off the block of ice you're standing on. Does that resonate with you?'

'Yes. The bit I'm on is big enough for now, but I'm not sure for how long, and it's drifting somewhere out of my control.'

'It doesn't sound safe or particularly empowered. Is that what you want to role model?'

Germaine laughed. 'I guess not.'

'So how does your purpose inform your decision?'

'That's a good question. If I'm a trust bringer I need to trust myself first. So I could say I trust that whatever happens is what's meant to be and everything will be fine. That would mean I don't need to do anything.'

'You don't sound like you believe that.'

'You're right. I know it's logical, but it feels like hiding,' said Germaine, amazed again at how perceptive he was.

'Great, you're listening to your intuition. How does that feel?'

'It's grounding to be open about that thought, no hiding. You know, the word that comes to me is stable.' Germaine laughed. 'I see what you're getting at: what appears to be no change is actually unstable, but stability comes from within.'

'Your insight, not mine,' Theo said.

'It's weird, but in the metaphor of the ice field everyone's on little blocks and we all need to hold together to stop it from drifting apart.'

'So who do you have to be to make that happen?'

Germaine laughed again. 'A leader who trusts myself and others and builds strong relationships.'

'Where are you leading people?'

'To the mainland, a place that's firmer, more supportive, where we can grow and it's easier to be balanced. You know, it's becoming clear that if I stay in my current role I can still hold things together and build trust in my team – we might even make it to where we want to go – but extending the metaphor, the MD role is like a big ship. It's there within reach; all I have to do is jump, be committed. With the ship we have more power to get where we want and it makes things so much easier for everyone. I just need courage to take it on and learn how to steer it. I might fail, but it seems silly not to take the risk.'

Germaine was getting into the analogy. Thinking of Mike again, she added, 'We'd have to watch out for abandoned ice blocks and pick our path carefully.'

'How does it feel to be at the helm?'

'Exposed but good. I wouldn't be alone, I couldn't do it alone.'

'What if you leaped and didn't reach the boat?'

'That would be OK. We'd still be afloat. I know those around me would help me out and we'd make it somehow.'

'Are things clearer now?'

'Absolutely,' she said. 'I really love this creative way of problem solving.'

'So what will you do? What action are you going to take?'

'I'm going to tell Jeremy that I want the MD role.'

'I hear a but,' said Theo.

Germaine laughed. 'Yep, it's got to be on certain terms. I need support, both from team members and Jeremy. I need to be able to try it my way and I need openness, transparency from the top down.'

'So when are you going to do it?'

'Tomorrow. Why wait?'

~ 42 ~

It was dark when Germaine woke up. A glance at her alarm clock told her she had half an hour before it was due to go off. Despite her excitement the night before, she had managed to go to bed at a reasonable time and had slept well. She didn't feel tired.

Ben was breathing deeply next to her. She contemplated waking him for some early-morning exercise, but he looked blissful and she didn't have the heart to disturb him.

She crept out of the bedroom, journal in hand. She could hear Barney's tail thump on the floor in recognition of her approach. It was too early for his breakfast and that was probably the only thing that would get him off his bed at this time. Weird, he was like Ben in so many ways. She got down to the dog's level, cuddled him and ruffled his ears, then retreated to the sofa.

Opening a new page of her journal, at the top she saw an illustration of a humming bird. She always loved the little images and wondered what the meaning behind them was.

She started to picture herself talking to Jeremy in his office, how she would feel talking to him and how he might react. Then she started to write in her journal, letting the words flow in a stream of consciousness. That hadn't been natural when she first started journaling, but now she really enjoyed it. She let the words flow and didn't worry about them making sense.

'I guess that's what life's like,' she wrote, 'you try something new and it feels a bit awkward at first, then after a while if you persist and relax, you find your way and it feels more natural. Perhaps that's a message for me going forward. So I will be open, straightforward and myself, I will accept if things are awkward and just relax.'

She made herself a cup of tea and sat quietly listening to the sounds of the house and the street. The world was waking up.

When she arrived at work, Tom asked if she would have lunch with him.

'I'd love to, but can I check my emails first in case there's something I need to attend to?' she said.

'Of course, I just want to catch up properly. You know, with you and what's going on here.'

Remembering what Jeremy had said, she thought about Tom's circumstances. She knew he must be aware that something was happening and that he was not being involved. She wondered why he wasn't pressing Jeremy for answers, but she knew all too well that feeling of insecurity, where you feel your destiny is at the whim of others. That had been her not too long ago, and she had a clear realisation of how far she had come.

Checking her emails, she saw what she was looking for, a response from Jeremy to her email of the night before:

I'm in at 9:30. You available then?
Jeremy

She was about to reply but then her mobile rang.

'Hi, Germaine,' Jeremy said. 'I thought it would be better if we talked outside the office. I'm five minutes away. Perhaps Dixies? Or Cafè Nero by the tube?'

'Fine by me,' she replied. 'See you in Dixies in 5.'

She breathed deeply and told Katherine she was popping out for a bit. 'I don't think I'll be longer than half an hour, but you can call me if it's urgent.'

Walking into Dixies, Germaine got a lovely feeling of being at home. Stefano came out from behind the bar when he saw her and gave her a big hug.

'It's lovely to see you,' he said. 'I was worried when your guys said you were ill, are you OK?'

When Jeremy entered he stood unnoticed, a spectator to this show of affection.

Stefano had introduced a new range of juices and smoothies in her absence and insisted she try the house special. He informed her it had been created by his eldest son. 'It's heaven in a glass, and it's good for you,' he said proudly.

Finally Jeremy managed to order a coffee and steer Germaine to a table.

'I hadn't realised we had a celebrity in our midst,' he smiled. 'You not being around for a while really brought it home what you contribute. Anyway, I assume you've thought about our conversation?'

Germaine nodded. 'This is it,' she thought. 'Here goes... Open and straightforward.'

'I would love to take on the MD role,' she told him. There, she'd said it.

Jeremy smiled again. He looked like a man who'd been given a coveted toy.

'However, I would need assurances. I have to do it on my own terms,' she added.

Jeremy frowned slightly, leaning back. Germaine could see he was waiting for the catch.

'I will need your guidance and support,' she told him. 'It's a big step and I will have blind spots and development areas that will need to be addressed. Having said that, I know I have enough strengths to compensate. But I will need to be able to make key decisions about the running of Copia without deferring to you. I can't be a puppet MD.'

She looked at Jeremy's face for a clue to how he felt. He wasn't giving much away.

'Go on,' he said. 'I'm listening. That's what being the MD is about.'

'I need to be the one who makes decisions on how we operate, how we deliver results, and to influence or even control the setting of strategic and financial goals. I'm talking about autonomy.'

'I hear you, but it's outside what I can commit to. Copia is not totally in our control any more. Ultimately it's the shareholders' decision.'

'But they also gave you assurances that the company would be autonomous for a couple of years, didn't they?'

Jeremy nodded, obviously weighing things up in his mind.

'I need you to be completely transparent with me, Jeremy. For this to fly, that is totally non-negotiable.' Germaine could feel the steel in her voice – not as a weapon but as a tool for getting things done.

'I did get that assurance, but I know in business that doesn't necessarily hold water,' he told her. 'Circumstances change. If we don't deliver on our promises or what's expected of us, then they will have a duty to act. I'm not sure about hitting them with any radical changes that might affect our ability to deliver. They're buying a successful company with great people, in a niche that complements their current offerings. You as MD and me as chairman guiding the company along its current path would be the continuity they're looking for.'

She could feel they were agreeing on the words, but something wasn't quite being communicated clearly. There was a principle involved.

'I need to build a relationship with the board and to be able to present my ideas even if they conflict with yours,' she insisted. 'I will be totally transparent with you and I need you to be so with me. You have skills and experience that I don't and may never have, but I am also confident that together we can take Copia on to the next level.'

As she said that, she realised it was exactly what she believed.

Jeremy seemed impressed. 'You know, I'm seeing a hardness that I haven't noticed in you before, in a good way. That's going to be vital. I will be honest now and say I had been viewing you as a safe transition, an easy way out for me, but hearing your desire and your determination, I believe we could make the company into something new and exciting.'

He seemed to be thinking out loud, realising his feelings as he spoke. 'I do think we can make it work. Let's put it to the main board, but I don't think it's going to be a problem.'

~ 43 ~

Later that morning Jeremy came over to her desk, his face beaming.

'I spoke to Steve and he said it's a goer. He didn't take any convincing, simply asked what I thought and agreed on the spot.'

Jeremy had forwarded her some emails containing important information about the deal, and she knew Steve was the group chief executive.

'Let's grab a conference room,' Jeremy added, pointing to the nearest one.

When they'd sat down, Germaine began, 'I still want to talk to Steve and the board. I need to have that relationship.'

'Of course, but I have to say that so far, my experience of dealing with them has been liberating. I'll see if I can get you along to see them this week. With that settled, we should have our own meetings to let everyone else know what's happening. Let's see if we can get a board meeting this afternoon and then the company meeting tomorrow.'

'Do you think that would give Tom and Mike time to get on board? It's not much notice to rearrange diaries.'

'I think it's important enough that people will have to. There are rumours going around anyway and delaying it any longer is going to cause problems.'

Germaine thought for a moment and added, 'OK, let's have the company meeting in the afternoon, as I'd like to talk to my team beforehand.'

'Sounds fine by me.' Jeremy smiled. He looked refreshed all of a sudden.

'Does Mike know about this? Have you any more idea what his role is going to be?'

'Not really,' admitted Jeremy. 'He's been keeping himself busy. It's your decision now. He might not be happy staying as operations and financial director, especially as I imagine much of the financial stuff will be migrated up to group level.'

Germaine realised she'd been tensing her hands, worried about how Mike was going to react. 'Shall we call him for a chat now?' she suggested. She didn't relish the idea, but she knew it was better to face the issue and deal with the consequences rather than hide and get a nasty surprise later.

Jeremy tried Mike's mobile number, but he wasn't picking up, so he sent a text asking what the FD's availability was. He got an immediate response from Mike and read it out loud: 'Personal matter, back tomorrow. If important email me.'

'That's curious, I bet he's got an interview.' Jeremy looked more amused than anything else, but then he frowned. 'I hope he's not muddying the waters for us. I think he might be pissed off that he wasn't in charge of the negotiations. He can't complain, though, he's getting more than he asked for.'

'If he won't talk to us, let's send him an email,' Germaine suggested. It felt good to be taking action. Whenever she felt tense or overexcited she told herself to relax; she took a few moments to breathe and remind herself what she was trying to achieve.

As they composed an email to Mike, Germaine noticed that Jeremy got straight to the point. Everything was represented as a fact, as if it had been agreed and was the only way. She would have been more inclined to explain the process and the thinking behind the decision and to invite Mike to present his own view. This realisation was enlightening in itself and was an indication of how they would need to adapt to each other's working styles in the future.

~ 44 ~

Germaine returned to the office to seek out Tom for their promised chat.

'Do you mind if we walk and talk?' she asked, feeling the need for some fresh air.

As soon as they were outside the building Tom piped up, 'So what's going on? You're all buzzing around and I feel like I'm being shut out. Mike has alluded to structural changes, but said he couldn't tell me yet. Jeremy's just been avoiding me.'

'Sorry about that, I think you should have been in the loop,' she said. 'Copia has been sold. It's a done deal and the rest of the company is being informed tomorrow.'

Tom looked genuinely surprised and a little hurt. Remembering how she had felt when she'd found out Jeremy was contemplating selling months ago, she felt a swell of compassion for him, as well as a little guilty.

'How long have you known, Germaine?' Tom murmured.

'I didn't find out about the sale till yesterday. Everything's been a bit of a blur. That's not the whole story, though. I did discover months back that Jeremy was looking to sell, but then a lot of other things happened.'

'Of course, sorry,' Tom replied. 'It wouldn't have been your priority given what was going on for you. I shouldn't be putting you on the spot.'

'That's OK. Even so, I feel I should have let you know,' she said. 'The thing is, I'm going to take on the MD role as part of the changes.'

'What's happening to Jeremy? Are you sure you want to do this given what you've just been through?'

'Yes, I'm sure. I'm not saying it's not daunting, but I know it's something I want to do.'

'So how do I fit in?' Tom asked, stopping for a moment. 'Am I part of the plans or am I for the chop? Is that why people are avoiding me?'

'That's certainly not the way I would like to start off,' Germaine said, resuming their walk. 'This is a great opportunity, and not just for me. All of us get a shot at creating what we want. I want you to be a big part in it, but it's up to you how much of a role you want to play. People love you, Tom, they confide in you, they like to work with you. You're wise and a great team player. You can carry on as before, but what I really want is for you to look at what you want to do and for us to collaborate to make that happen.'

Tom looked thoughtful as he walked. 'How will that work? It's not as if there's a shortage of things to do around here.'

'Let me share my experience,' she said. 'A lot of my energy used to be focused on the wrong things. But then I realised that as long as we're focused on the right things, there will always be time for the things we love. For instance, I always said I couldn't have a dog as it would be too time consuming, but that was just an excuse. Since we got Barney, our golden Labrador, he's fitted into our lives perfectly.'

Tom was nodding. 'Maybe I shouldn't be saying this, but recently I've thought about going back to college to do psychology or perhaps an MBA.'

Germaine got a sudden tingle of excitement and stopped, looking Tom in the eye. 'It just came to me that you could be a brilliant coach. I think your greatest strength is people – you're interested in them, you care about them, and they know it. It would be incredibly useful if you could coach people here, helping them to bring more of themselves to work and be more balanced.'

Tom looked excited too. To walkers passing by they probably seemed like lovers discussing a holiday, an adventure. They both felt the excitement of new possibilities.

'I'd love to do something like that, but how could we make it happen?' Tom was looking to her for answers.

'I don't know, those are the kind of details we have to work through. The point is, we have an opportunity. Can I count on your support? You can count on mine.'

'Of course, Germaine. You're an inspiration to me – and not just to me but the company.'

They turned back to the office and the conversation moved to what Germaine was going to do first. She confided that she'd been considering who she should promote to client services director, Katherine or Owen. She had already discounted recruiting externally for the role, even though that might have been an easier decision for her.

Tom was surprisingly sure of himself. 'I'd choose Owen, no question.'

Germaine had been leaning that way, but felt a strong loyalty to Katherine. She had always disliked the fact that it was easier for men to rise to leadership positions and she didn't want her first actions as the boss to perpetuate that particular status quo.

'He's more ready, more mature, more balanced,' Tom counselled. 'Katherine's more like you were a couple of years ago: smart, great at her job, good with people. Owen has all of that to a greater or lesser extent, but he has more gravitas. I wish I had some of his poise.'

Germaine knew what he meant as soon as he said it. 'Yes, self-assurance.' She remembered that was the attribute that had made her feel insecure around Owen in the past. He had what she felt she had lacked at that time. She was more self-assured now and could appreciate the quality in others. Just like that, her decision had been made.

~ 45 ~

Owen took the news in his stride and accepted the job in principle, pending a formal offer and a couple of other conditions. He really did seem unflappable. He offered Germaine his help in whatever way he could in the meantime.

The conversation with Katherine was a little more difficult.

'Copia has been sold,' Germaine began. 'We'll still be largely autonomous, but we're taking the opportunity to reorganise ourselves for the future. Jeremy will have a more strategic advisory role, more of a chairman really. He's asked me to take the position of MD. I think you can appreciate that it's a big step for me. As part of my decision I needed to feel I'd have the support of Jeremy, the new owners and most of all my team.'

Germaine paused to see how Katherine was taking the news. She looked tense and was frowning, but she showed no intention of interrupting.

'I know I have a great team,' Germaine continued. 'Each member of it has their own strengths and together we pull out all the stops to get the job done. There are two people who stand out as being capable of moving up to client services director, you and Owen. You're both incredibly talented, in fact you have more potential and ability than I did when I was given the position.'

She could tell from the look on Katherine's face that she had guessed what was coming.

'You have a lovely way of building rapport with those around you. You have a head for the bigger picture and can step in and do the detail. People like to work with you, Katherine.' Germaine laughed, consciously breathing out to release any tension she was feeling about the conversation. '*I* love to work with you and to be perfectly honest, in the past I've sometimes felt a bit threatened by you. You're bright and innovative and you have all the attributes to be an incredible leader – you just need to believe in yourself. Katherine, I see such gifts in you, but I don't think you're ready yet and I don't think giving you the job would be the best thing for you.'

Katherine looked deflated and as if she was struggling to contain competing emotions.

'It wasn't an easy decision,' Germaine went on, 'but my instinct told me Owen was better suited to the position at this moment in time. However, his condition for taking on the role was that you were OK with it.'

On a whim, she added, 'It took me a while to get clear on what I really wanted and I know coaching helped. Perhaps it might be good for you too. We could arrange for you to meet Theo or a different coach if you think it might be useful.'

Katherine seemed to pick up on that idea. 'I think I'd like that. If I'm honest with myself, I'm not sure I'd have wanted the job just now, but I can't say I'm not disappointed.'

'I understand totally. I would have been the same in your situation. In hindsight I really should have been having these conversations anyway, but I was caught up in the day-to-day stuff and to be honest I avoided things like succession planning.'

'It's OK, you've been holding a lot, even before your break.'

Germaine thought 'break' was an interesting description, but she acknowledged that Katherine was right. 'Yes, I think that was part of the problem. I was holding it all too tightly.'

~ 46 ~

Tom and Mike were talking when Germaine arrived. Tom looked up at her with raised eyebrows, and she wasn't sure what to make of that.

'Where are Jeremy and Dominic?' she asked.

'Jeremy's on his way, but I don't know about Dominic,' Mike replied coolly.

Right on cue, Jeremy bundled through the door holding a take-away coffee cup. 'Dominic couldn't be here, he's out of town, but we're going to get him on a conference call.' He went to the phone and dialled the number.

'Dominic Fox,' the speakerphone announced.

'Right, now we're all here we can begin,' Jeremy said. 'You may have seen the email about the company meeting later today. As I think you all know, Copia has been acquired. It's an exciting opportunity for us all. Dominic, myself and Mike have been working in the background to make sure the deal is good for Copia and its clients.'

He hooked up his laptop to the overhead projector and proceeded to go through the structure of the deal they had negotiated, then went through Dunston Capital's presentation of the group strategy and how Copia fitted into their plans.

'Steve was due to do this part of the presentation, but he can only make the company meeting this afternoon. He apologises, but to be fair I didn't give him much notice,' Jeremy explained. 'To be honest I wouldn't have gone into so much detail about the deal, but our new MD insisted on transparency.'

Germaine could feel herself blushing.

'Let me introduce her formally. Germaine, would you like to say something?'

She was nervous, despite it being the same team she had talked to on a daily basis for the last few years. 'We've taken Copia from a tiny ten-man operation to a thriving agency, winner of many awards,' she began. 'We've been an incredible team and we've managed to recruit some fantastic talent. I feel that Jeremy is spot on, we're at the start of an exciting journey. It's not all mapped out, but at least we now know what's expected from us in terms of the numbers.'

'Can you tell us how those numbers were derived, Germaine? Are they reasonable?' Mike interrupted her flow, his face blank. He'd lit the touch paper and he leaned back in his chair with his arms folded.

Thrown off track, Germaine looked briefly at Jeremy. It seemed as if he was going to come to her defence when suddenly he flapped his arms. 'Shit, there's a wasp in here, where did that come from? I hate those bloody things.' He swatted it with a remarkable backhand, then stepped on the insect on the floor.

Germaine breathed, using the distraction to collect herself. 'Just be yourself,' she thought.

When Jeremy had sat back down, she resumed her presentation. 'You know, Mike, you're right. I don't know where those figures came from. Perhaps I should have found out before I accepted the position, but you know, for me trust is a big thing and I needed to make a quick decision. And since you and Jeremy were in charge of the negotiations, I trust that you have done the right due diligence. So I'm curious as to the purpose of your question.'

Mike remained tight-lipped and gave nothing away.

'The point you were trying to make might have been valid,' she continued. 'I do need to be more focused on the numbers and it's an area I need to develop. However, it's the way you asked the question that leaves me feeling as if you don't want to collaborate with me. What I want to see is the company pulling together more, not less, so that we can succeed both as individuals and as an agency and be happy in the process.'

She glanced around to see Jeremy smiling and the others nodding. Mike just looked at her.

'Hear, hear. Put that in your pipe and smoke it, Mike,' Dominic piped up from the speakerphone. That caused a round of laughter and released the tension.

They carried on talking through their plans and how the company meeting was likely to go. Germaine felt in her element, canvassing opinion and facilitating the discussion. She couldn't help noticing that the others listened more and that both Mike and Jeremy now took more of a back seat.

When she left the boardroom she felt as if the dynamics of the team had shifted and she had finally taken her place. She was proud of herself and her heart was almost bursting out of her body as she acknowledged: 'This is it. This is my time.'

Resources and Recommended Reading

EFT (TAPPING)

EFT (Emotional Freedom Technique) is an energy psychology tool that is a relatively new western application of something based on very ancient practices. With physical tapping at specific points along our energy meridians, EFT 'taps' into our energy system to balance it and keep it running smoothly.

www.emofree.com

THE STRESS MANAGEMENT SOCIETY

The Stress Management Society is a not for profit organization dedicated to helping people tackle stress.

www.stress.org.uk

RECOMMENDED READING

The Journey, Brandon Bays (Thorsons, 1999). An inspirational story where the author shares how she healed herself physically and designed a powerful approach that has helped thousands of people the world over. www.thejourney.com

Emotional Intelligence, Daniel Goleman (Bantam Doubleday Dell, 1996). This highly regarded book by psychologist Daniel Goleman explores what Emotional Intelligence is, how it can be developed, why it's crucial and some of the neuroscience behind it.

MIndfulness: A Practical Guide to Finding Peace in a Frantic World, Mark Williams and Danny Perryman (Piatkus, 2011). This book explores some of the secrets of inner peace and details a unique programme developed by Oxford University psychologist Professor Mark Williams.

Authentic Success, Robert Holden (Hay House, 2011). An inspiring book that explores what it means to be truly successful across all areas of your life, in a way that is heartfelt and soulful.

I Will Not Die an Unlived Life, Dawna Markova (Conari Press, 2000). This powerful book is a testament to the power of choice that we all have. The author demonstrates how we can all live with more passion, power and purpose.

Making the Big Leap, Suzy Greaves (New Holland, 2010). Acclaimed life coach Suzy Greaves offers an invaluable guide in the form of exercises, practical help and stories to inspire the reader to move towards creating the life they desire.

Co-Active Coaching, Henry Kimsey-House, Karen Kimsey-House, Philip Sandahl & Laura Whitworh (Nicholas Brealey, 2011). One of the most comprehensive books for teaching the skills of coaching using the co-active approach. A must-have for any aspiring coach.

The Power of Now, Eckhart Tolle (Namaste Publishing, 1999). A classic book that draws on a variety of spiritual traditions and portrays the benefits of living in the present moment and how liberating that can be.

The Suited Hippy Series

If you would like to receive new book release information for the Suited Hippy series or Suited Hippy special offers, please subscribe to our mailing list at:

http://eepurl.com/Or3pb

If you enjoyed or hopefully gained something from reading this book, please review it on Amazon and/or recommend it to a friend.

Printed in Great Britain
by Amazon.co.uk, Ltd.,
Marston Gate.